REFORMATION, EXPLORATION, AND EMPIRE

Volume 2

CATHOLIC CHURCH–DAILY LIFE

GROLIER

an imprint of

█SCHOLASTIC

www.scholastic.com/librarypublishing

Published by Grolier,
an imprint of Scholastic Library Publishing,
Sherman Turnpike
Danbury, Connecticut 06816

© 2005 The Brown Reference Group plc

Set ISBN 0-7172-6071-2
Volume 2 ISBN 0-7172-6073-9

Library of Congress Cataloging-in-Publication Data

Reformation, exploration, and empire.
    p. cm.
    Contents: Vol. 1. Academies–Catherine de Médicis —
v. 2. Catholic church–daily life — v. 3. Decorative arts–
fortifications — v. 4. France–inventions and inventors —
v. 5. Ireland–manufacturing — v. 6. Maps and
mapmaking –Orthodox church — v. 7. Ottoman Empire–
printing — v. 8. Privacy and luxury–sculpture — v. 9.
Servants–textiles — v. 10. Thirteen Colonies–Zwingli.
    Includes bibliographical references and index.
    ISBN 0-7172-6071-2 (set : alk. paper) — ISBN 0-7172-
6072-0 (v. 1 : alk. paper) — ISBN 0-7172-6073-9 (v. 2 :
alk. paper) — ISBN 0-7172-6074-7 (v. 3 : alk. paper) —
ISBN 0-7172-6075-5 (v. 4 : alk. paper) — ISBN 0-7172-
6076-3 (v. 5 : alk. paper) — ISBN 0-7172-6077-1 (v. 6 :
alk. paper) — ISBN 0-7172-6078-X (v. 7 : alk. paper) —
ISBN 0-7172-6079-8 (v. 8 : alk.paper) — ISBN 0-7172-
6080-1 (v. 9 : alk. paper) — ISBN 0-7172-6081-X (v. 10 :
alk. paper)
    1. History, Modern—16th century—Encyclopedias,
Juvenile. 2. History, Modern—17th century—
Encyclopedias, Juvenile. 3 Renaissance—Encyclopedias,
Juvenile. 4 Civilization, Modern—17th century—
Encyclopedias, Juvenile. 5 Reformation—Encyclopedias,
Juvenile. I. Grolier (Firm)

D228.R46 2005
909'.5'03—dc22   2004063255

For information address the publisher:
Grolier, Sherman Turnpike,
Danbury, Connecticut 06816

FOR THE BROWN REFERENCE GROUP

Project Editor: Emily Hill
Deputy Editor: Tom Webber
Designer: Joan Curtis
Picture Researcher: Susy Forbes
Maps: Darren Awuah
Design Manager: Lynne Ross
Production Director: Alastair Gourlay
Editorial Director: Lindsey Lowe
Senior Managing Editor: Tim Cooke
Consultant: Prof. James M. Murray
                           University of Cincinnati

Printed and bound in Singapore

ABOUT THIS SET

This is one of a set of 10 books about the key period of western history from around 1500 to around 1700. The defining event of the age was the Reformation, the attempt to reform the Catholic church that resulted in a permanent split in western Christianity. The period was also marked by the European exploration and colonization of new lands, profound political change, and dynamic cultural achievement.

The roots of the Reformation lay in a tradition of protest against worldliness and corruption in the Catholic church. In 1517 the German Augustinian monk Martin Luther produced a list of criticisms of Catholicism and sparked a protest movement that came to be known as Protestantism. The reformers broke away from Catholicism and established new Protestant churches. In response the Catholic church launched the Counter Reformation, its own program of internal reforms.

Religious change had a profound political influence as Protestantism was adopted by various rulers to whom it offered a useful way to undermine Europe's existing power structures. The period was one of intolerance, persecution, and almost continuous warfare. Meanwhile new approaches to religion combined with the spread of printing and increased literacy to produce a knowledge revolution in which new ideas flourished about science, art, and humanity's place in the universe.

Changes in Europe had a lasting effect on events elsewhere. Spanish conquistadors overthrew vast empires in the Americas, while Catholic missionaries spread Christianity in Africa, the Americas, and Asia. Gradually lands in the east and the west were penetrated and colonized by Europeans. These and other important changes, such as the development of international trade, great cultural achievements, and the spirit of learning, are explored in detail in each volume.

While focusing mainly on Europe, the set also looks at important developments across Africa, Asia, and the Americas. Each entry ends with a list of cross references to related entries so that you can follow up particular topics. Contemporary illustrations give a fuller picture of life during the Reformation. Each volume contains a glossary, a "Further Reading" list that includes websites, a timeline, and an index covering the whole set.

Contents

Volume 2

CATHOLIC CHURCH

In 1500 the Catholic church was the one unifying feature of western Europe. During the 16th century, however, attempts to reform the church led to conflict and the eventual division of western Christianity between Catholicism and Protestantism.

The western Christian church split permanently in two when an attack on church abuses by a German monk, Martin Luther, in 1517 developed into a wider movement for change known as the Reformation. Protestants, as those who protested against the Catholic church came to be known, broke away and established separate reformed churches.

There had been reform movements in the Catholic church before. In the 13th century a spiritual revival was led by Saint Francis of Assisi and Dominic

Representatives of the Holy League, formed by Pope Pius V to fight the Ottoman Turks in 1571, kneel before him in Rome.

Guzman. They founded orders of friars, who took strict vows of poverty and obedience and went out into the world to spread the word of God in reaction to the growing wealth and worldliness of many monasteries.

Some calls for reform had been condemned as heretical (going against the teachings of the church) and had been suppressed by the Inquisition, a religious court established in 1231. Among the first victims were the Waldensians, founded in France in the 12th century. They were followed in the 14th century by the Lollards, whose leader, the Englishman John Wycliffe, attacked the corruption and wealth of the church. Wycliffe greatly influenced the Czech reformer Jan Hus, who was burned at the stake in 1415.

PAPAL AUTHORITY

In 1500 the Catholic church was in crisis. The pope's authority had been seriously undermined by the Great Schism of 1378 to 1417. During the schism two men—one based in Rome and the other in Avignon, France— both claimed to be pope. Although the schism was ended by the Council of Constance, it had done a great deal to discredit the papacy's claim to represent the authority of God on earth.

The conciliar movement, which began in 1409 with the aim of healing the Great Schism, tried to establish the principle that general councils should meet regularly to institute reforms. The popes saw the conciliar movement as a threat to their own power and resisted convening councils for reform. As a result, an important opportunity for the church to reform itself was missed.

CHURCH ABUSES

During the Renaissance of the 14th and 15th centuries a series of popes behaved more like secular princes than

spiritual leaders, attracting more criticism. They flouted church laws, such as the requirement to remain celibate, and became notorious for their great wealth and luxurious way of life. Several popes appointed their friends and relatives to high positions in the church, regardless of whether or not they were qualified for the post. One of the outstanding examples was Pope Alexander VI (pope 1492–1503). He had several children and made one of his sons, Cesare Borgia, a cardinal at age 18. Cesare was famous for his cruelty and extravagance. Both he and Alexander were suspected of being involved in several murders.

In 962 the pope had crowned the first emperor of the Holy Roman Empire, aiming to create a powerful secular deputy to rule Christendom.

In this painting from the 1520s Saint Ursula stands reading from the scriptures while relics of another saint arrive at a church in Lisbon, Portugal. There were many cults of saints throughout Europe, and Catholic believers enthusiastically collected their relics, such as bones or hair.

In this woodcut by Hans Holbein Pope Clement VII (pope 1523–1534) presides over the sale of indulgences.

He had, however, created a rival. From the 11th century the pope and emperor struggled over the right to appoint bishops and the control of lands in Italy. The papacy's desire to extend the Papal States, the area over which it had direct control, led to Alexander VI encouraging a French army to invade

Italy. His successor, Julius II (pope 1503–1513), organized a coalition of states, the Holy League, to fight the French. Such actions did little to raise the prestige of the papacy.

Abuses were not confined to the popes; they were found throughout the church hierarchy. Positions in the church were bought and sold, and pluralism (the practice of holding several posts at once) was widespread. At the bottom of the hierarchy many parish priests were both very poor and poorly educated. Many knew barely enough Latin—the language used by the church and educated people—to recite the Mass.

REFORMING POPE

When Paul III (pope 1534–1549) was elected, he seemed little different from previous popes; for example, he made his two teenage nephews cardinals. However, he appointed a commission to report on the state of the church. The commission's 1537 report was extremely critical of the papacy, the clergy, and the religious orders. In 1545 Paul III finally responded to the

PURGATORY AND INDULGENCES

Catholics believed that after death a person's soul went to purgatory, where it would be purged of sin before going to heaven. It might, however, never be purged of sin and so would end up in the fires of hell that were so graphically illustrated in many church paintings. There was no agreement about whether anything could be done on earth to reduce the amount of time spent in purgatory. Indeed, some people believed that nothing could be done at all. However, at the beginning of the 16th century it was generally thought that celebrating Mass, making regular confessions, and performing charitable deeds would all help. People could also purchase indulgences from the church. These were documents that could reduce the penance or punishment not only for their own sins but also for the sins of those who had already died and whose souls were in purgatory. The sale of indulgences enabled the church to increase its already considerable wealth but became a powerful symbol of the church's corruption.

challenge posed by the Protestants by calling a reforming council.

The Council of Trent met over 20 years and achieved important reforms. It reorganized the church, strengthened discipline, emphasized the importance of training clergy and preaching, and clarified and reaffirmed the church's traditional teachings. The council's decisions were conservative and left little or no possibility of reconciliation with the Protestants.

THE COUNTER REFORMATION

The Council of Trent was part of a movement known as the Counter Reformation, the internal reforms that reinvigorated the church from the later 16th century, reversing many of the gains of Protestantism.

A new religious order, the Society of Jesus (the Jesuits), was responsible for much of this success. The Jesuits were called the "shock troops of the Counter Reformation" because of their dedication to reviving church life and their military-style discipline. They were very active, especially in education, founding universities, schools, and colleges. They traveled all over Europe and far beyond to win converts, and had success in Europe, in Spanish and Portuguese colonies in the Americas, and in East Asia. A new artistic style, the baroque, expressed the emotion and drama embodied in the Counter Reformation's religious ideas. Many new churches were built or old ones remodeled, notably Saint Peter's, Rome.

RENEWED CONFIDENCE

The threat of invasion by the Muslim Ottoman Turkish Empire had long cast a shadow over Europe. In October 1571 the Holy League, an alliance of European states led by the pope, was victorious over the Turks at Lepanto. Although little changed politically as a

result of the battle, the victory was a great boost to Christian morale.

The end of the Thirty Years' War (1618–1648) saw increased religious toleration in Europe. The Catholic church was now only one of a number of Christian churches, and there were several challenges to the reduced authority of the church later in the 17th century. States—in particular France— tried to restrict the pope's involvement in running national churches.

In addition, a popular movement known as Jansenism, for the Dutch religious thinker Cornelius Jansen, criticized the direction the church had taken during the Counter Reformation and specifically opposed the Jesuits. In the 18th century they were gradually expelled from French, Spanish, and Portuguese territories. The pope suppressed the order in 1773.

The cathedral of Saint James in Santiago de Compostela in Spain was a major pilgrimage center. Protestants criticized the popular Catholic practice of going on pilgrimages.

SEE ALSO
- Clergy
- Counter Reformation
- English Reformation
- Inquisition
- Luther, Martin
- Papacy
- Reformation
- Religious dissent
- Religious orders

CENTRAL ASIA

From 1500 to 1700 Central Asia was dominated by two empires centered on the cities of Bukhara and Khiva in modern Uzbekistan. As global oceanic trade routes developed overland, trade routes through Central Asia became less important, and the region lost significance.

Central Asia occupies a vast area in the heart of Asia bounded by the Caspian Sea in the west and the Tian Shan Mountains in the east, the Siberian forest in the north, and the Hindu Kush Mountains in the south. The landscape is mainly made up of the steppe (open plain), desert, and high mountain ranges, but there are also many fertile river valleys.

In 1500 the region had many rich and ancient urban centers. These cities had grown wealthy because of their location on the Silk Road, a network of trade routes linking Europe and East

Asia. The region was also home to thriving agricultural communities in the fertile valleys and many different nomadic tribes who roamed the vast pasturelands of the steppe. From the time of the Arab conquest in the seventh century A.D. Islam was the dominant religion in Central Asia.

RIVAL KHANATES
In the 16th and 17th centuries two rival areas controlled by a ruler called a khan (khanates) were the main powers in Central Asia. They are generally known by the names of their capital

The view from the Kunya-Ark fortress, which guards the ancient city of Khiva, Uzbekistan. Khiva was one of the most important cities in Central Asia in the 17th century.

CENTERS OF LEARNING

The ancient urban centers of Bukhara, Khorezm, and Samarkand, which became prosperous from their locations on the trade routes linking Europe and Asia, also became centers of Islamic learning. In these cities lived and worked great Islamic scientists and poets. In the 16th century these Central Asian cities, together with Tashkent and Qokand, remained important centers of Islam and commerce, but they gradually became less prosperous. New trade routes by sea reduced the amount of goods traded overland. At the same time, Central Asia lost ground to expanding empires: China in the east, Mogul India and Safavid Persia (Iran) in the south, and Russia in the north and west.

Medressa Tella in Samarkand, Uzbekistan, was a theological school for young men. During the 16th and 17th centuries they came from around Uzbekistan to this school to be instructed in Islam.

cities, Bukhara and Khiva. The ruling elite in both khanates were Uzbeks, nomads who had risen up and wrestled power from the descendants of the great Central Asian ruler Timur (1336–1405). The Uzbek khans ruled over many different peoples both nomadic and settled, including Uzbeks, Tajiks, Kirgiz, Turkmens, and Karakalpaks.

The Bukhara Khanate was set up by a group of Uzbeks led by Shaibani Khan, who took over Timur's capital, Samarkand, at the start of the 16th century. In the 1530s they moved their capital to Bukhara. The khanate fought the Moguls in India and the Safavid Dynasty in Iran. In addition it often fought the rival Khanate of Khiva.

The Khiva Khanate was established in 1511 when a rival group of Uzbeks conquered a region on the Amu Darya River. Khiva became the capital in the early 17th century. A period of stability brought economic progress, and major irrigation projects were undertaken. Uzbek tribes settled on irrigated lands granted by the government.

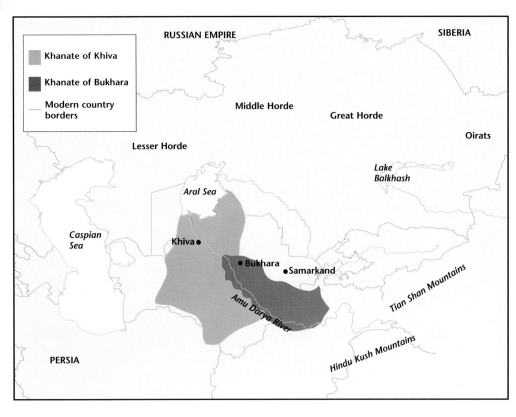

Map legend:
- Khanate of Khiva
- Khanate of Bukhara
- Modern country borders

Map labels: RUSSIAN EMPIRE, SIBERIA, Middle Horde, Great Horde, Oirats, Lesser Horde, Lake Balkhash, Aral Sea, Caspian Sea, Khiva, Bukhara, Samarkand, Amu Darya River, Tian Shan Mountains, Hindu Kush Mountains, PERSIA

This map shows Central Asia in the 17th century. The khanates of Khiva and Bukhara were the centers of power in the region. Kazakh nomads lived in groups called hordes in the pasturelands between the Caspian and Aral seas and Lake Balkhash. They often clashed with the khanates and their archenemies the Oirats, who lived in the east.

The political fortunes of Bukhara and Khiva depended on their relationship with the nomadic peoples of the steppe: The Turkmens and Karakalpaks in the east, the Kazakhs in the north, and the Oirats in the east. These nomadic peoples were organized in loose tribal confederations that were in a state of constant warfare with each other and the khanates. If the ruler of a khanate failed to pay tribute to a tribal chief, raids against the khanate's towns and villages immediately followed, and the main cities often fell into the hands of the nomadic armies.

KAZAKHS AND OIRATS

In this period the most powerful nomadic groups were the Kazakhs and the Oirats. Both lived mainly by raising herds of sheep and horses on the steppe. Both were famous for being fine horsemen and formidable warriors.

The pasturelands of the Kazakhs stretched from the Caspian Sea to Lake Balkhash and were divided among three "hordes" (groups), each ruled by its own khan. According to Kazakh tradition, their common ancestor divided them into three groups under his three sons of different ages, to which the names of the groups correspond: the greater, the middle, and the lesser hordes. From 1680 to 1718 one khan, Tauke, united all Kazakh hordes. During this period the Kazakhs adopted a written law code as a sign of their authority. Although the Kazakhs were Muslims, the new code was based on their customary laws.

In the 17th century the Oirats, the Kazakhs' greatest enemies, who occupied a territory east of Lake Balkhash, inflicted a series of crushing defeats on the Kazakhs.

From the late 1700s the expanding empires of Russia and China began to encroach on the nomads' pasturelands. They ended the strategic importance of the nomadic armies, leading to the Russian imperial conquest of much of Central Asia in the 1800s.

SEE ALSO
- China
- India
- Islam
- Persia
- Russia
- Trade

CHARLES V

Charles V (1500–1558), Hapsburg king of Spain and Holy Roman emperor, ruled the largest empire in Europe. He faced numerous religious, political, and economic challenges during his reign, but his chief concern was resisting the spread of Protestant ideas.

Born in Ghent in what is now Belgium on February 24, 1500, Charles was the son of Philip "the Handsome" of Burgundy and Joanna "the Mad." Charles inherited a huge empire from his grandparents, Maximilian I (1459–1519), Holy Roman emperor, Ferdinand of Aragon (1452–1516), king of Spain, and Isabella (1451–1504), queen of Castile. Charles inherited territories across Europe including parts of the Netherlands, Austria, Switzerland, the southern half of Italy, and Spain, along with Spain's American colonies. In 1519 Charles was elected Holy Roman emperor to maintain loose authority over a confederation of lands in western and central Europe.

CHARLES'S EMPIRE

By the age of 20 Charles ruled a vast empire. Unable to be everywhere at once, he employed deputies, often family members, to rule in his place. Throughout Charles's life his brother Ferdinand had an important role in the running of the Hapsburg Empire.

Charles met his challenges with varying success. One of the earliest was the demand for reform in the Catholic church led by Martin Luther. In 1521 Charles, who was a devout Catholic, presided over the imperial diet, or council, at Worms in Germany, where Luther defended his position. Charles strongly rejected Luther's ideas.

Although Charles was determined to counteract Luther's influence in Germany, he faced other pressing problems. He was fighting for supremacy in Italy against King Francis I of France (ruled 1515–1547). In the battle of Pavia in 1525 French forces were defeated by the Spanish army, and Francis was captured. He was forced to sign the humiliating Treaty of Madrid in 1526, in which he handed lands in Italy and Burgundy to Charles.

A portrait of Charles V riding his horse dating from 1519. It was painted by the 16th-century Venetian artist Titian.

However, when Francis was released, he immediately broke his word. He formed the League of Cognac with northern Italian city-states and Pope Clement VII. Charles reacted by sending an army to Italy. They defeated the league and sacked the holy city of Rome in 1527, an event that shocked Europe. Thousands of Romans died, and the pope was forced into hiding for several months.

Charles faced a constant threat from the Islamic Ottoman Empire of Turkey. The Turks under Suleyman the Magnificent (ruled 1520–1566) occupied Hungary in 1526 after defeating the king of Hungary at the Battle of Mohács. They were poised to expand deeper into Europe and reached as far as Vienna in 1529 but then retreated.

In the 1530s North African pirates sponsored by the Turks attacked Spanish ships. In 1535 Charles captured Tunis in North Africa, but at the naval battle of Prevesa in 1538 the pirate fleet beat Charles and his allies, establishing Turkish control of the eastern Mediterranean. Despite Suleyman signing a peace treaty with Charles in 1544, war between the Ottoman Empire and the Hapsburgs continued to rage long after Charles died.

WINDING DOWN

Charles funded his campaigns by heavy taxation, selling titles and lands, and taking out loans from the Fuggers, a German banking family. The costs of running the Hapsburg Empire were substantial, and by the end of Charles's reign it was in enormous debt. Charles's financial problems, his failing health, and his disappointment at failing to suppress Protestantism led to his gradual withdrawal from power.

In the early 1550s Charles turned over control of Germany and later much of the Hapsburg Empire to his brother Ferdinand. He abdicated control of the Netherlands and Spain to his son Philip II in 1555 and 1556 respectively. Charles then retired to a monastery in Yuste in Spain, where he died in 1558.

A 16th-century painting showing Charles V surrounded by his enemies.

SEE ALSO

- Council of Trent
- Dynastic wars
- Fugger family
- Hapsburg family
- Holy Roman Empire
- Italian Wars
- Luther, Martin
- Ottoman Empire
- Reformation
- Rome

CHILDREN

In the 16th and 17th centuries life for many children remained similar to life in previous centuries. However, the period was also a time of changing attitudes toward children: Humanist and Protestant ideas emphasized the roles of families and schools in the raising of children.

Throughout the period the social status of a child's parents generally determined the course of his or her life. Children of the nobility tended to learn skills including poetry, music, dancing, and for boys, hunting and the use of weapons; girls were married off at a young age. Girls from wealthy nonnoble families also married early, but boys often received further education in schools and the increasing number of universities. This formal education prepared them for careers as civil servants, doctors, lawyers, or clergymen. Sons of craftsmen usually apprenticed or trained in their father's trades, while their sisters might enter domestic service as servants.

LABOR AND POVERTY

Children of poor parents were expected to contribute to their family's upkeep. From the age of six or seven this involved simple tasks such as looking after younger siblings or scaring birds off crops. When they were older, children took on heavier labor. Working conditions could be harsh, but many children were able to combine work with play. Young shepherds in 16th-century Spain, for example, mingled their flocks of sheep so that they could play games with other shepherds.

Death was an everyday fact of life. Approximately 20 to 25 percent of children died before age four; death

rates among parents were also high, resulting in a great number of orphans. Orphans and other poor vagrant children often formed gangs, to the disapproval of many adults who accused them of theft and general mischief. Vagrant children were also put in orphanages known as foundling hospitals. These hospitals were usually set up and run by the church. By 1700, however, more were being established by local councils and funded by charitable donations.

THE IMPACT OF NEW IDEAS

The spread of humanist ideas from the 1400s influenced the treatment of children. They emphasized the dignity and worth of individuals. Humanists such as the Dutch scholar Erasmus (about 1466–1536) held that fathers

Las Meñinas *by the 17th-century Spanish artist Diego Vélazquez. The painting dates from 1656 and shows the daughter of King Philip IV of Spain being attended to by her maids of honor. In the 17th century children of both noble families and nonnoble families were dressed from an early age in an adult fashion.*

had the primary responsibility for their children. This differed from the traditional notion that mothers had the crucial role in a child's upbringing. Erasmus also stressed that an early education later made a model citizen.

RELIGION AND CHILDREN

The religious beliefs of parents also shaped their attitudes toward children. Protestants and Catholics both believed that humans were born into a state of sin, but Catholics believed that infant baptism helped cleanse children of their inherited sins. Both religions regarded discipline as an important form of education for children. Catholics and Protestants argued that among the important values in children were piety, or respect and obedience. The Counter Reformation—the Catholic church's response to criticism of its doctrines and to the spread of Protestantism—led to the belief that schools rather than families should be responsible for raising good Christians. New Catholic religious orders such as the Jesuits, established by Spanish priest Ignatius Loyola (1491–1556) in 1539, dedicated themselves to the education of young children. A famous Jesuit saying embodied their values: "Give me a

child until he is seven, and I will give you the man." During the 16th century Jesuits were sent on missions across Europe and in the Americas to establish schools for children and non-Christians.

This woodcut from 1524 shows an early German school where pupils are seated according to their ages. The teacher sits between the two groups, reading at a lectern.

PARENTAL LOVE

Many social historians believe that the harsh conditions in which people lived during the 16th and 17th centuries meant that parents did not love their children in the way with which we are familiar today. Often parents regarded children as economic assets or unprepared adults who would later have a useful role in society. Poor parents, for example, expected children to work for them; some historians believe that they may not have been devastated about offspring who died young because infant mortality was common in the period. Other historians believe that parental love—and love for one's parents—has always existed. They argue that such love was expressed in many ways, most of which revolved around children providing for their parents. Children were also proud to work for their parents, forging a loving relationship based on their ability to help.

SEE ALSO

- Families
- Humanism
- Jesuits
- Reformation
- Schools and schooling
- Social order
- Wealth and poverty

CHINA

Europe had little contact with China before 1500. As contact increased between 1500 and 1700, European explorers sought to discover a sea route to China to avoid the high costs of overland trading. The Catholic church also extended its influence by sending missionaries to China.

In 1500 China was ruled by the Ming Dynasty. The Ming had come to power in 1368, replacing the Mongols, and continued to rule until 1644. They established a strong government and a population of more than one million in territory that included much of modern China. The Ming period was highly prosperous. Porcelain manufacturing became a thriving industry, and Chinese merchants explored the Indian Ocean. China established contact with Africa through the voyages of the Chinese explorer Cheng Ho (about 1371–about 1433). By 1500, however, the government had outlawed voyages beyond imperial borders and made it illegal to build oceangoing ships. As a sign of China's increasing fear of outsiders, the Great Wall was reinforced with cannons and improved watchtowers to keep foreigners at bay.

Europeans had made direct contact with China in the 13th century, when the brothers Nicolo and Matteo Polo and Nicolo's son Marco traveled along the Silk Road from western Asia. The Silk Road was a trade route through Central Asia. The Mongols who controlled

A 16th-century Ming dynasty porcelain vase. Its colored glazes and floral design are typical of the period.

the route allowed the Polos and other European traders to travel through their territory. Few others used the route, however, because it was so long, and there were many dangers along the way, including deserts, treacherous mountain passes, and bandits. The Ming closed the Silk Road to foreigners as part of their attempt to make China self-sufficient and independent. The decline of contact did not lessen the popularity of exotic Chinese goods for Europeans, however. Fine porcelain, silks, and spices continued to make their way from East Asia to Europe by both land and sea. European merchants relied on trade with middlemen from Arabia, Egypt, and elsewhere to supply their customers.

By the late 15th century the Spanish, Dutch, Portuguese, and English were funding expeditions hoping to be the first to reach Far East Asia via a western sea passage. Genoese explorer Christopher Columbus originally thought he had reached Japan when he sighted the Bahamas in 1492. Although he was soon proved wrong, he and other explorers

THE MANDARINS

Ming emperors ruled with the help of a class of officials called Mandarins. To work for the Chinese government was a very desirable high-status job. To become a government official, candidates for civil servants or commanding positions in the military had to pass a competitive exam, so boys started their education at a young age. The exams often lasted several days, and the only way to pass was to commit whole books to memory. Emphasis was put on rote learning and the ability to quote relevant passages of Confucionist literature. Confucionist philosophy, based on the work of the ancient Chinese philosopher Confucius (551–479 B.C.), emphasized ritual, hierarchy, and obedience to the state. Students succeeded who respected the state system and had an excellent education and well-developed memories. The emphasis on tradition meant that people working for the state were loyal to the Chinese Emperor.

A stone sculpture portraying a typical military official (left) and civil official during the Ming Dynasty (1368–1644).

continued to search for a sea passage to China, which they believed lay just beyond the newly discovered islands.

THE PORTUGUESE IN CHINA

By the mid-17th century China was beginning to renew contact with the outside world. It lifted the ban on oceangoing ships and resumed trade with Europe. When the Portuguese reached India by sea in 1498, they established trading colonies and began to follow Indian trade routes toward China. They were among the first Europeans to reenter the Chinese Empire. In 1517 the Portuguese reached China and sent a mission to Beijing led by Tome Pires, a doctor who later became the Portuguese ambassador to the Ming court.

The Portuguese discovered that the Chinese had a radically different view of the world from their own. The Chinese believed that their emperor ruled from the heart of the civilized world. Any foreigner wanting to see the emperor had to perform a series of tributes and kow-tow, or bow, to acknowledge the emperor's greatness. Foreign merchants, missionaries, and government envoys had to bring gifts for the emperor. The emperor gave

This Ming dynasty silk painting shows female Chinese musicians. The Chinese were the first people to master the production and weaving of silk. It was expensive to make, and only wealthy members of Chinese society could afford it. Large quantities of silk were exported to Europe.

gifts in return to demonstrate China's economic and cultural supremacy. The Chinese regarded the ceremonial exchange of gifts as a sign that the foreigners accepted the superior status of China and its ruler. Although the emperor accepted the tributes of the Portuguese emissaries, he refused them the right to return. The official Portuguese mission returned to Beijing only in 1670.

TRADING IN MACAU

In 1557 Chinese officials allowed the Portuguese to found a trading colony in Macau, on the southern coast of China. In return for the right to set up warehouses and lodgings for merchants the Portuguese helped the Chinese stop pirates from terrorizing the coast. At Macau the Portuguese bought Chinese porcelain, silks, spices, and tea to ship

to Europe. The Portuguese were not allowed to travel inland from the enclave and were closely regulated so that they did not set up trade on their own but worked only through the traditional channels provided by Chinese officials. The Chinese were not interested in buying European goods, which they considered to be inferior to their own.

The Portuguese used Macau port to import goods from other regions and then to export them without paying taxes or duties. Portuguese traders also brought in goods from Japan, some of which they sold to the Chinese. They controlled important commercial links between China and Japan from 1543 to 1639, and imported cargoes of goods from both nations to Europe. Other European nations soon realized the potential profits of trading in China.

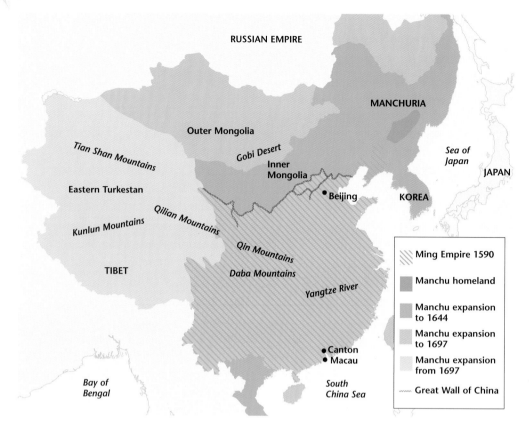

A map showing the Ming Empire in around 1590 and the different stages of Manchu expansion in China during the 17th century. In 1644 the Ming Empire collapsed, and by 1700 the Manchus ruled vast territories in China.

At the beginning of the 17th century the Dutch and the English both fought with Portugal over Macau.

MISSIONS TO CHINA

Merchants were not the only Europeans interested in visiting China. With the Portuguese traders came Catholic missionaries. Between 1552 and 1583, 32 Jesuits and a number of Franciscans and Dominicans attempted to set up missions in China. Most were never allowed past Macau or the city-province of Canton in southeastern China, where the Portuguese sent an embassy in the 16th century, followed by the English and Dutch in the 17th century. Those who were allowed usually only stayed for a short time.

At first Christian missionaries encouraged their Chinese converts to give up Chinese dress and to follow European laws and customs. Chinese officials resented this practice since it suggested that Chinese culture was inferior. Later, missionaries relaxed their attitudes, adopting Chinese dress themselves and respecting Chinese customs. Francis Xavier (1506–1552), a missionary who helped establish Christianity in India and Japan, advocated that missionaries should adopt the language and customs of the people who are being converted. The work of early missionaries in China such as Matteo Ricci (*see box p. 20*), Michele Ruggieri, and Francesco Pasio was continued by later generations of Catholic missionaries, but by 1700 there were very few Chinese converts.

THE MANCHU

In 1644 the Manchu, a group of people from northeast China known to the Chinese as the "eastern barbarians," conquered Beijing and overthrew the Ming Dynasty. By 1680 the Manchu ruled all of China under the name of the Ch'ing Dynasty. When the Manchu came to power, they decreed

MATTEO RICCI

Matteo Ricci (1552–1610) was an Italian Jesuit who arrived in China in 1582. His aim was to convert the Chinese to Christianity, but he knew that he would have to behave very carefully since the Chinese treated foreigners with great suspicion. First he spent his time learning the Chinese language. In 1583 he and a fellow Jesuit priest, Michele Ruggieri, set up residence at Chao-king, the capital of Canton, and gained the support of local officials. At first Ricci and Ruggieri did not preach but told the Chinese that they had come to China because of its great reputation. They initially attracted people's interest by demonstrating clocks, maps, a painting of Mary and Jesus, and other items of European culture, and gradually won the trust of the Chinese. By 1584 the two Jesuits had printed a book in Chinese containing the main points of Catholic doctrine. In 1588 Ruggieri returned to Europe, and in 1589 Ricci was expelled from Canton because the governor of the region claimed Ricci's house. Ricci had made many friends, however, and was able to visit other cities. He then worked his way toward Beijing, the capital of the Ming Empire. In 1601 Ricci was summoned to the capital by the emperor. Ricci spent his last nine years in Beijing. He gave the emperor gifts, including a European map of the world, and impressed the Chinese court with his knowledge of science and astronomy and his command of the Chinese language. Matteo was the first foreigner to be allowed to live permanently in Beijing. He died there in 1610. His work later led to Emperor K'ang-hsi permitting Christians to preach throughout China from 1692.

A 17th-century illustration of the Jesuit priest Matteo Ricci, left, with his first Chinese convert.

that the Chinese had to wear their hair in a pigtail as a sign of submission.

In the 17th century the Manchu Emperor K'ang-hsi (ruled 1661–1722) extended China's influence abroad. He was an exceptional leader and a talented military tactician. During his reign the Chinese Empire expanded to include parts of what are now Russia, Mongolia, and Tibet. He encouraged the introduction of European culture and the teaching of Catholicism.

The Manchu were enthusiastic patrons of Chinese art and culture, although they also tried to keep Manchu customs separate from those of the Chinese to preserve them. They were not successful, however, and gradually in China Manchu and Chinese cultures became intermixed.

SEE ALSO

- Central Asia
- Jesuits
- K'ang-hsi
- Missionaries
- Portugal
- Tea and coffee
- Textiles

CHRISTINA OF SWEDEN

Christina (1626–1689) was queen of Sweden from 1632 to 1654, when she abdicated in favor of her cousin Charles Gustavus. Intelligent and well educated, she was Europe's most celebrated convert to Catholicism. After her abdication she spent most of the rest of her life in Rome.

Christina was born on December 8, 1626, in Stockholm. The only child of King Gustavus Adolphus of Sweden and Maria of Brandenburg, she was raised as a boy.

Christina inherited the throne in 1632 aged six, when her father was killed in battle. A council of regents ruled on her behalf until she was 18. During her early years as queen she helped bring about the end of the Thirty Years' War (1618–1648).

Christina invited many scholars, writers, and artists to her court, including the French philosopher René Descartes (1596–1650). She refused to marry, calling marriage a "horrible yoke." Despite her intelligence and ability as a monarch, she failed to improve Sweden's precarious finances.

Christina abdicated in 1654 in favor of her cousin Charles Gustavus. She formally converted to Catholicism and went to live in Rome.

An equestrian portrait of Queen Christina of Sweden painted by her French court painter Sebastien Bourdon (1616–1671).

LIFE IN ROME

In Rome Christina was the center of society. Her behavior, however, caused controversy. She involved herself in politics instead of living quietly and fell in love with a cardinal, Decio Azzolino.

In 1662 she moved into the Palazzo Riario, where she built up a fine art collection of works by contemporary masters, including the Italian artist Gian Lorenzo Bernini (1598–1680). She had a large library and founded an academy and a theater, the first public institution of its kind in Rome. She died in 1689 and was buried in Saint Peter's basilica in Rome.

SEE ALSO

- Bernini, Gian Lorenzo
- Courts and courtiers
- Descartes, René
- Gustavus Adolphus
- Scandinavia
- Thirty Years' War

CLERGY

Clergy are officers of a religion. In the Christian church they have been ordained or commissioned as ministers to perform special functions, such as preaching and administering sacraments, such as the Lord's Supper, also known as Mass or the Eucharist.

In 1500 the clergy in the Catholic church was organized in a strict hierarchy with the pope at the head of the church. The pope lived in Rome, supported by a large staff. The most important were the cardinals. They were the pope's principal advisers and elected each succeeding pope from among their number. Some cardinals lived mainly in Rome, while others were archbishops in their own countries and visited Rome only occasionally.

Bishops were key members of the Catholic clergy. One of their most important roles was to ordain or appoint priests. The pope appointed a bishop to run an area called a diocese. A bishop had total religious authority in his diocese, although the pope had power to remove a bishop from office. For each group of dioceses there was an archbishop—a bishop who had extra powers and responsibilities over the whole area, not just his own diocese. In England, for example, there were two archbishops, at Canterbury and York.

Monasteries and religious orders sometimes tried to bypass the local bishop's control by placing themselves directly under the pope's authority.

A 17th-century woodcut showing a parish priest administering the sacrament of the last rites to a dying man. Administering the sacraments was one of a priest's most important duties.

A 15th-century panel showing a bishop celebrating Mass with clergy. Celebration of Mass, or the Eucharist, became a central area of argument in the Reformation. Leading reformer Martin Luther argued that every Christian, not just ordained priests, should be allowed to receive both the bread and the wine at the Eucharist.

Depending on the religious order they belonged to, the monastic community might be secluded in a life of prayer or might provide friars who traveled the country preaching. Other communities ran schools or hospitals.

PARISH PRIESTS

A diocese was organized into a number of parishes, each run by a parish priest who was primarily responsible for leading the faithful to God. The local priest had to live a virtuous life, be celibate (remain unmarried), hold church services, and visit the sick. His most important duty was to administer the sacraments. As one of the few local people who could read, he helped others with the writing of wills and other legal matters, and ran reading and writing classes for children in his house.

In Europe priests usually came from poor rural parishes similar to those that they served. The priest therefore understood the people. If the parish was poor, then so was the priest, reliant as he was on tithes (a tenth of the local income). Priests grew even poorer when it became common practice for unscrupulous tithe-collectors to retain some of the money.

WIDESPREAD RESENTMENT

By the 16th century many people felt considerable resentment toward the clergy. First, the clergy enjoyed special privileges: They did not have to pay taxes and were subject to a less harsh justice system than ordinary people. People also increasingly viewed the church hierarchy as an obstacle rather than a means to reach God.

Another cause of resentment was the poor quality of parish priests, especially in rural areas. Some priests hardly knew Latin well enough to perform services, while others could not even read. The poverty of parish priests often gave them a low status in local communities.

Further up the church hierarchy there were abuses such as pluralism (the holding of several different posts at the same time) and simony (the buying and selling of church offices). Many bishops were extremely wealthy, in stark contrast to the poverty of most ordinary members of the church.

EFFECT OF THE REFORMATION

The Reformation called into question the role of the clergy. A central Protestant belief was that a priest was not needed to help people go to heaven. An individual's faith in God was enough for his or her sins to be forgiven and to be accepted into heaven. The Protestant reformers emphasized the idea of the "priesthood

of all believers"—that everybody had an equal status in the sight of God. Protestants and Catholics therefore saw the clergy very differently. While Catholics believed ordination gave the clergy a special character that set them apart for life, Protestants saw the clergy as essentially the same as other members of the church, even though they had a particular function.

ORGANIZATION OF CLERGY

The Protestant churches organized their clergy in different ways. Some, such as the Church of England, kept much of the Catholic structure. The Puritans, who emerged in the 1560s in reaction to the Church of England's political compromises, chose their ministers by democratic ballot. Scottish and Dutch Calvinists retained their ministers in the form of pastors elected by church elders. Sects such as the Mennonites had preachers, elders, and bishops. But they shunned churches, instead worshiping in their own houses.

A portrait of John Michael Dilherr, a Protestant pastor in Nuremburg, Germany, who published two books of sermons. The Protestants emphasized the importance of good preaching.

FROM PRIEST TO PARSON

The Church of England, the English national church, was formed after the rift between Rome and Henry VIII (1509–1547), when Pope Clement VIII refused to grant Henry a divorce from his wife Catherine of Aragon. At Henry's insistence Parliament passed a series of acts that culminated in the king becoming head of the English church (1534). While the monasteries were closed, much of the original church government was left in place. The Archbishop of Canterbury, together with various councils, was now responsible for running the church. One seemingly insignificant change revolutionized the church. Priests were no longer trained at the church's expense in seminaries but were expected to get a divinity degree at a university such as Cambridge, which had reformed its monastic houses into divinity colleges. From then ministers were limited to the sons of nobility and those merchants prosperous enough to pay for a university education.

The middle-class minister or parson was not expected to mix socially with his ordinary congregation and rarely if ever took their side in a dispute. If his parish or living was rich, he might live in London and hire a recently qualified minister to perform his parish duties. This unforeseen consequence of Anglicanism resulted in the formerly close relationship between the rural poor and their priest being lost forever.

SEE ALSO

- Catholic church
- English Reformation
- Papacy
- Puritans
- Quakers
- Reformation
- Religious orders

CLOCKS AND CALENDARS

By the 16th century astronomers and scientists were developing increasingly advanced clocks that accurately measured and kept time. At the same time, however, the Julian calendar, which had been in use for 1,600 years, was growing out of step with the passing of the seasons.

The clock would prove to be one of the most influential discoveries of western science. By providing the means to divide time into regular, accurate periods, it allowed society to develop toward a greater degree of efficiency and sophistication. Early clockmakers applied theories of physics and mechanics to making a clock. The principles of clock construction were understood by the ancient Greeks, but the technology to build a clock only became available in the 1300s. In the 1500s the most common type of clock was mechanical. It had a device for storing energy—either a spring or weights raised above the ground—that was regularly released into the machine parts in order to turn the hands or hand of the clock.

PUBLIC TOWN CLOCKS

The first clocks were large. Mechanical tower clocks first appeared in Italian cities in the 14th century. They were powered by a mechanism called a verge-and-foliot escapement, in which a T-shaped bar turned to engage and disengage a toothed wheel, called the crown wheel. The repetition of this action regulated the movement of the hands of the clock. Town clocks soon appeared all over Europe. They were not very accurate, however, and lost up to half an hour a day.

In about 1500 the German clockmaker Peter Henlein designed a clock powered by a spring. This breakthrough allowed clocks to become smaller and also enabled the production

The 17th-century Dutch scientist Christiaan Huygens. He first used pendulums to regulate the timekeeping of clocks.

of the first portable clocks, later called watches. Henlein's original clocks only had an hour hand; the minute hand did not appear until 1670. By 1530 most people relied for timekeeping on the chiming of the church or town clock. Wealthy people who owned a clock did not at first live their lives by clock time, however: Clocks were still a novelty and were not always accurate.

During the 16th century clock designs became elaborate. Clockmakers across Europe competed to create unique clocks in a variety of forms such as animals. Artistic styles such as the baroque influenced clock design. In addition to telling the time, intricately designed clocks also included dials that showed presumed movements of the planets. Valuable materials like gold and silver were combined in expensive clocks. In some clocks metal figures were connected to the timekeeping mechanism so that they danced and acted at the stroke of each hour.

CHRISTIAAN HUYGENS

In 1656 Dutch scientist Christiaan Huygens (1629–1695) made the first pendulum clock, possibly working from a design by the Italian scientist Galileo Galilei (1564–1642). Huygens used the pendulum's natural motion to create timepieces that were accurate to within one minute a day. It was the first time such accuracy had been achieved. Huygens wanted to produce the world's most accurate clock, and within a few years he reduced the time error to less than 10 seconds a day. He later designed small clocks with a balance wheel and spring assembly, a design still used in wristwatches.

In the 18th century Huygens's designs were used to produce clocks that were accurate to one second a day. In 1761 British inventor John Harrison designed the marine chronometer based

LIFE WITHOUT CLOCKS

Before clocks were invented, most villages rang bells to announce the new day. Adjoining villages kept different times, however, so that it could be Wednesday in one village but still Tuesday in another.

Other than by observing the sunrise or sunset, there was no agreed time when a new day began. People organized time into weeks and months. There was a time for planting, a time for weeding the crops, and a time for harvesting. Days were identified by reference to activities such as taking produce and animals to the local agricultural fair. Sundays and religious holidays were days of rest. The idea of dividing days into hours seemed very strange at first. When French explorer Jacques Cartier (1491–1557) first landed in Canada, the indigenous peoples whom he met were amazed at the French clocks. They decided that there had to be a spirit within the clock, telling the colonists what to do.

A modern pendulum clock based on Christiaan Huygens's 17th-century design.

on Huygens's designs. The chronometer was accurate enough to enable navigators for the first time to accurately calculate their longitude, a relative east-west position on the globe.

GAINING TIME

By the 16th century it was clear that the calendar and the seasons were out of step. Each year the planting time for crops occurred earlier in the calendar. In a farming society such a misalignment was potentially serious. Farmers could not rely on the calendar to tell them when to plant and harvest their crops.

The Julian calendar then in use was named for its creator, Roman Emperor Julius Caesar (100–44 B.C.). He had set the length of a year at 365 days. He also made every fourth year a leap year, in which there were 366 days. However, the actual length of a year is 365.2422 days. Each year of the Julian calendar was effectively 10 minutes, 44 seconds too long. By the late 16th century this had added up to 10 days. In 1582 the first day of spring occurred on March 11 instead of the traditional March 21.

The Catholic church was determined to solve the problem. In 1514 Pope Leo X wrote to European monarchs seeking advice on how the calendar could be reformed. Both this letter and a second one written two years later received little response. However, Leo's second letter inspired Polish astronomer Nicolaus Copernicus (1473–1543) to address the problem. Copernicus recorded his theories about the calendar in his book *De Revolutionibus* (Concerning the Revolutions of the Heavenly Orbs), which was published in 1543. In the book he also argued that the sun was the center of the universe, rather than the earth, as argued by the the church. This meant that Copernicus's ideas achieved little acceptance, although they would

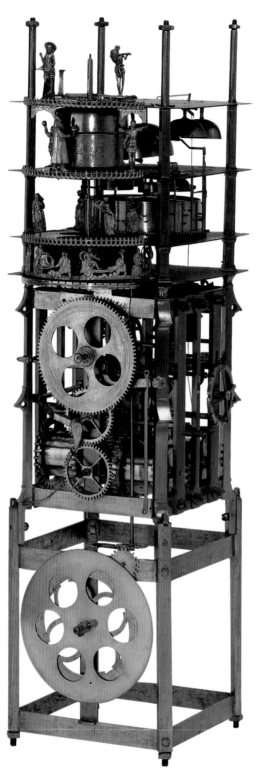

The mechanism of a carillon clock from 1589, which as well as keeping the time, also plays short musical pieces.

eventually influence calendar reform and dramatically change astronomy.

COPERNICUS'S LEGACY

Although Galileo Galilei recognized the importance of Copernicus's work, other astronomers and mathematicians were initially more interested in his theories on the movements of the planets and the length of the year. One of those who studied *De Revolutionibus* was Aloysius Lilius (1510–1576), a physician from southern Italy, who created a formula to reform the Julian calendar. However, Lilius's sudden death meant that his ideas were not immediately presented to Pope Gregory XIII (pope 1572–1585). The Jesuit astronomer Christoph Clavius (1537––1612) championed Lilius's manuscripts and gave them to Gregory's calendar commission. Lilius's solution was to drop 10 days from the calendar immediately and to restart the vernal equinox—when the sun passes north across the earth's equator, marking the start of spring—back to March 21. Lilius retained leap years, with the exception of century years, which in future would be leap years only when divisible by 400. So 1700, 1800, and 1900 were not leap years in the Gregorian calendar—named for the pope—but 1600 and 2000, both divisible by 400, were. The effect of the century leap-year rule is to drop three days from the calendar every

THE PROBLEM OF EASTER

The problem of calculating the true length of a year created a second problem for Pope Gregory XIII—fixing the date for Easter, the most important Christian festival. The problem arose because witnesses to Christ's death and resurrection had not recorded the date. The Council of Nicaea (325 A.D.), an assembly of bishops who reaffirmed Christian doctrines, attempted to solve the problem with a formula: Easter Sunday would be the first Sunday following the first full moon after the vernal equinox (March 21). They referred to the moon because Jewish holidays were calculated using the lunar calendar. Calculating the true date for Easter required the lunar calendar to be synchronized with the solar calendar. Previously this had been done using as a reference point the Metonic Cycle, in which the lunar and solar calendars coincided every 19 years. By contrast, Aloysius Lilius calculated that the lunar calendar drifted from the solar calendar at a rate of one day every 312.7 years. He suggested a correction cycle that begins by dropping a day from the lunar calendar every 300 years; this is done seven times, and then, on the eighth occasion, a day is dropped after 400 years. Along with other corrections Lilius's system is still used today.

400 years, effectively eliminating the accumulation of additional time in the Julian calendar.

CALENDAR CHANGE

On September 14, 1580, the commission handed its official report to Gregory XIII, who enthusiastically endorsed the plan, although it was not implemented until 1582. Gregory chose October as the month for adjustment, because that meant fewest feast days would be lost. People throughout Europe went to sleep on October 4, 1582, and woke on October 15. Pandemonium broke out as crowds rioted in Rome and Frankfurt, accusing the church of stealing 10 days of their lives. In response, European governments passed laws to adjust contract dates and to ensure that landlords did not collect a full month's rent for October.

Protestant countries were slower to change their calendars, the Netherlands making the change in 1700. Britain and its American colonies delayed the change until 1752.

The papal bull signed by Pope Gregory XIII in 1582, authorizing reform of the calendar.

SEE ALSO
- Copernicus, Nicolaus
- Papacy
- Science

COLONIAL WARS

Establishing colonies overseas increased the wealth and power of many European countries, but it also caused numerous wars. There were two main types of colonial conflict: Wars fought by local people against the colonial power, and wars fought between colonizing countries.

Between 1500 and 1700 colonial wars raged primarily in three regions: the Americas, Africa, and Asia. In the Americas Spanish and Portuguese forces were the first to use military might to colonize. At the beginning of the 16th century the Spanish had more advanced weapons than the Native Americans. They used muskets, cannons, and superior ships to dominate larger foreign armies.

Although the Spanish and Portuguese established large empires in the Americas, maintaining their colonies was not easy. During campaigns to conquer Guatemala, Honduras, the Yucatán, and Brazil native peoples resisted European forces, fighting long wars and killing many Europeans.

In addition, from the mid-16th century Spain and Portugal's American colonies were increasingly raided by English, French, and Dutch forces. In 1568 Spain attacked English shipping in the Caribbean. In response Francis Drake, England's leading naval commander at the time, sent naval expeditions along the coast of the Americas. Drake intercepted Spanish convoys transporting silver back to Spain and raided Spanish harbors. From 1585 the two countries were effectively at war. Spanish ships traveling between the West Indies and Spain were constantly attacked by English vessels. Drake launched

a particularly devastating assault on Spanish settlements in the Caribbean in 1585. Spanish and English naval conflicts ceased in 1604 when peace was reached in the Treaty of London.

NORTH AMERICAN WARS
In North America there was conflict between English and French colonists and Native Americans. The English established 12 large colonies along the east coast, but they faced opposition from local Native Americans who

A 17th-century illustration of Nipmuc Native Americans from Massachusetts attacking an English settlement in King Philip's War (1675–1676). Fighting broke out after the English kidnapped a local chief.

violently resisted losing their land. From the early 1600s many Native Americans had firearms. In 1622, for example, a raid by Native Americans on Virginia killed around 350 Europeans, and in New England wars raged with local peoples from 1675 into the 1700s.

Although France fought against Native American peoples, mainly the Iroquois, they also allied with some groups. The French responded to raids by destroying Native American villages and arming rival tribes. However, in the 1640s an Iroquois tribe called the Mohawks crushed the Huron, Nipissing, and Petun tribes—allies with the French who had fought alongside the French against other Native Americans. From 1658 the Mohawks attacked French forces directly. The French responded by nearly wiping out the Iroquois between 1666 and 1697. Iroquois survivors were forced to accept a settlement in 1701; but following the agreement, they suffered further defeats at the hands of the English.

English and French forces also fought each other. In 1629, for example, the English took over the French city of Quebec, but in 1632 the French won it back. In 1713 the English made inroads into New France, part of the Americas claimed by the French. They took over Nova Scotia, an area called Acadia initially settled by French colonists. Warring between European colonial powers in the Americas continued into the 18th century.

AFRICA AND ASIA

In Africa and Asia the dominant colonial powers were Spain, Portugal, and the Netherlands. The Europeans had few actual colonies; most of their settlements were trading posts and harbor towns. Portuguese dominance along the African coast and across

KING WILLIAM'S WAR

Conflict in the colonies often mirrored political alliances and rivalries in Europe. In the 17th century English and French colonies competed for control of the profitable fur trade in North America. Religious tensions already existed: French colonists were mainly Catholic, while English colonists were mostly Protestant.

In England the Catholic King James II tried to restore Catholicism as the official religion in England but fled to France when his efforts failed. James's daughter Mary and her husband William of Orange became the English monarchs in 1688 at a time of great change known as the Glorious Revolution. The Catholic king of France, Louis XIV, who was sheltering James, refused to recognize the new English monarchs and declared war on England. This war was echoed in the Americas, where it was known as King William's War because of the controversial English king. Fighting between English and French colonies was marked by a series of massacres of colonists by Native Americans allied to both European countries. In 1697 a peace treaty signed by the English and French failed to settle the dispute, which erupted in further wars during the 1700s.

the Indian Ocean was contested by several nations. For example, in the early 1500s Egypt wanted to curb the spread of European Christian influence. Egypt clashed with Portugal

A 16th-century illustration of French colonists building a fort in the Americas.

in the Indian Ocean during various naval battles, defeating the Portuguese at Chaul in 1507 but suffering defeat at Diu off northern India in 1509.

TURKISH INTERVENTION

The Ottoman Empire absorbed Egypt in 1517 and sent its navy to defeat the Portuguese. Although the Ottomans devastated the Portuguese base at Muscat on the coast of Oman in 1552, the Portuguese triumphed at Ormuz in a naval battle two years later. During the course of the 16th century, however, Portuguese naval superiority gradually diminished. In East Asia China defeated Portuguese ships off Tunmen in 1522, and in 1575 the Portuguese lost the trading base of Ternate in the Moluccas Islands to a local dynasty. Between 1598 and 1663 the Dutch also captured several major Portuguese territories in East Asia and along the coast of India.

Spain became powerful in North Africa during the early 1500s, controlling some of what are now Morocco and Algeria. However, local Muslims turned against the Spanish, and in 1529 Ottoman forces of Suleyman the Magnificent pushed the Spanish out of Algiers and from Tunis in 1534. In response Charles V of Spain led a crusade against North Africa. Both sides suffered heavy losses, and war continued into the 1570s, by which time Spanish power in North Africa was confined to a small region in the northwest.

PORTUGUESE DECLINE

Portugal also faced challenges to keeping its territories in Africa, including Tangier and Ceuta in the north, and parts of Angola, Mozambique, and Mombasa in the east. Although the Portuguese had superior weapons, they struggled to

dominate. Most of the conflict took place in Angola and Mozambique. In 1644 Portuguese forces suffered a major defeat by Ndongo soldiers in Botswana. By the 1680s Portuguese and Ndongo armies had fought to a stalemate. In 1631 people from Mombasa revolted against Portuguese rule and stormed Fort Jesus, a Portuguese outpost. It was later reclaimed, but in 1698 it was taken by Oman, an emerging Arabian empire. Portugal also had problems with other colonizers. The Dutch, for example, took four Portuguese African settlements from 1637 to 1641, which the Portuguese fought to reclaim.

A painting from 1697 depicting a naval battle between Ottomans and the Portuguese off Ormuz in the Persian Gulf.

SEE ALSO

- Colonization
- Conquistadors
- Exploration
- Ottoman Empire
- Spanish Empire
- Trade

COLONIZATION

The 16th and 17th centuries were an age of European colonization. Europeans began to establish settlements and later gain political power in new lands. By 1700 the Americas were largely under European rule, and colonies existed as far east as Japan.

Colonization refers to the process by which a country settled and exploited a foreign territory. Between 1450 and 1700 Europeans colonized most of the Americas and small areas of India, East Asia, and Africa. The main motivation for colonization was trade, but imperial expansion and religious conversion were also important. Europeans profited by selling domestic goods in the new markets and by bringing exotic commodities to Europe. These commodities included silver from South America, fur from North America, gold from Africa, and spices from East Asia.

European colonization became possible in the early 1500s thanks to improvements in military and maritime technology and navigation. Accurate methods of measuring latitude became available from the 1460s, more reliable compasses were invented, and the Portuguese and Spanish developed sturdy and maneuverable three-masted ships called caravels capable of long sea voyages. Gunpowder weapons such as muskets and cannons put Europeans at an advantage over the people of the territories that they colonized.

PORTUGUESE TRADERS

In 1500 there were two main European colonial powers, Spain and Portugal. In the late 15th century both countries had explored the oceans in search of new trade routes to Asia. The Portuguese explorer Vasco da Gama made an epic voyage in 1497–1498 from Portugal to India. He opened up new trade routes, and the Portuguese established settlements in Africa from 1505, in India in 1510, in what is now Malaysia in 1511, and at Macau in China in 1557.

These settlements were trading posts rather than colonies. Macau, for example, was only founded with the permission of the Chinese authorities. The Portuguese ruled these settlements under their own laws, and in some African settlements they even made

A recreation of Jamestown, Virginia, the first permanent English settlement in North America. Jamestown was founded in 1607. Its location in an unhealthy, marshy area led to a high number of deaths from disease.

local people pay taxes. The Portuguese controlled maritime trade routes to Asia in the 16th century from their harbors in the Indian Ocean.

SPANISH CONQUESTS

Sponsored by Queen Isabella of Spain (1451–1504), Christopher Columbus reached the Americas in 1492. He set up a small colony on an island near Cuba, which he named Hispaniola. This first Spanish colony was a failure—when Columbus returned in 1493, he found the colonists had all died. However, by 1510 Spanish settlements were established on the mainland in Panama, and from there they spread into South America. The Spanish also started to explore northward into North America.

Spanish colonization was frequently violent. Small numbers of Spanish soldiers known as conquistadors took over much of the Americas against larger local armies, winning battles with their advanced weapons and spreading European diseases such as smallpox

that devastated native populations. In 1521, within two years of arriving in what is now Mexico, Spanish forces had overcome the Aztec Empire. Between 1531 and 1533 Spanish conquistadors overthrew the Inca Empire in Ecuador and Peru. They destroyed most native villages, towns, and cities, founding Spanish settlements in their place. By 1600 the Spanish Empire in the Americas stretched from Mexico down to Chile and on the east coast of North America around Florida and the Caribbean islands.

DEVELOPMENT OF COLONIES

Many early European settlements were small coastal trading posts protected by a garrisoned militia. By the 1700s these settlements had become permanent fortified colonies, often with a Christian mission, and were home to thousands of inhabitants. In Brazil the Portuguese crown made its first efforts to establish a government in 1533, dividing the land along the coast into

This map shows European countries and the areas that they colonized between 1600 and 1700.

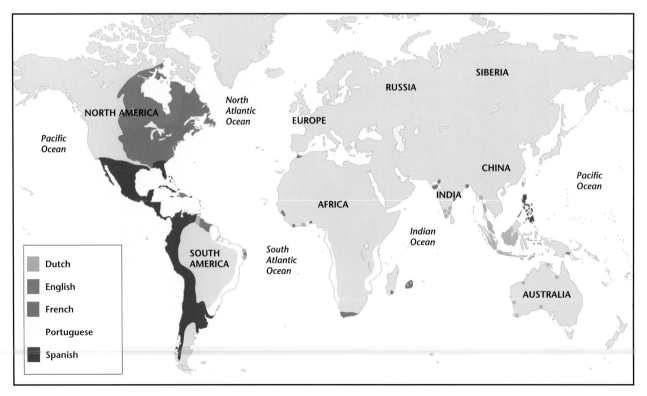

Dutch
English
French
Portuguese
Spanish

captaincies. During the next decade the Portuguese king appointed a governor to rule on his behalf. Coffee from plantations in northeastern Brazil meanwhile became a valuable import to Europe.

The American colonies generated massive wealth and resources for Spain. The labor for mining and agriculture was provided at first by local peoples. Under Spanish rule Central American peoples were organized into small working groups called *encomiendas*. The Spanish controllers largely ignored their obligation to protect these native peoples and educate them in Spanish customs and the Christian religion. The Indians were increasingly enslaved and forced to work to build and maintain new colonies. In practice many of the *encomiendas* were little more than slave camps.

ATTACKS ON SPAIN

Other countries—England, France, and the Netherlands—soon wanted to share in the wealth of the New World. Throughout the 16th century English and Dutch warships attacked Spanish merchant convoys crossing the Atlantic laden with treasure and raided harbors on the American coastline.

During the 17th century the English and Dutch built more ships and vastly increased their naval power. They formed trading companies that had royal authority to acquire foreign lands. The English East India Company, founded in 1600, and the Dutch East India Company, founded in 1602, set up global trading networks.

By the 1700s the English and the Dutch had acquired most of the islands in the Caribbean. The Dutch were more interested in taking over the Portuguese trading networks than establishing a continental empire. They only established two colonies, Cape

Town in South Africa in 1652 and New Netherland in North America in 1621, later captured by the English and renamed New York. Although the English and Dutch did not take any of Spain's mainland colonies, their presence in the Caribbean severely disrupted Spanish trade and led to a decline in the Spanish Empire.

NORTH AMERICA

France began its exploration of North America in the 16th century, founding its first successful colony at Acadia (Nova Scotia) in 1604. The French moved along the St. Lawrence River and around the Great Lakes, where they traded furs. By 1700 they had colonized the length of the Mississippi River down to the Gulf of Mexico, securing territories between the English and Spanish colonies. The French established many cities, including Quebec in 1609 and Detroit in 1701.

The English colonized North America from 1584, establishing the first permanent colony at Jamestown in Virginia in 1607. In 1620 the *Mayflower* carried English pilgrims to Massachusetts Bay, where they founded

A 17th-century stone church in Creel, northern Mexico, built by Jesuit missionaries. From 1521, when Spanish soldiers led by Hernán Cortés overthrew the Aztec Empire, Mexico was part of Spain's empire in the Americas.

RELIGION IN THE COLONIES

Early European colonizers believed they had a duty to bring Christianity to the new lands. When they reached the foreign colony, missionaries built churches and began to introduce Christianity to local people.

In some places this was easier than in others. For example, Spanish Jesuit missionaries in China initially found it difficult to overcome the language barrier and then had to adopt Chinese customs before their own faith was respected and eventually slowly began to be accepted.

While Christianity was often used as a way to control local peoples, some missionaries such as the Spanish Dominican monk Bartolomé de Las Casas dedicated their energies to protecting the rights of the native peoples. Las Casas also recorded details of the existing cultures, leaving a valuable record for future generations. Elsewhere, particularly in North America, colonies provided an opportunity for religious minorities to escape persecution. For example, the Puritans set up colonies in Virginia in the 1600s.

the first permanent colony in New England. Over the next 80 years the English established 12 large colonies along the eastern coast, including New York, which they had gained from the Dutch in 1664, and Delaware, which had originally been settled by Swedes. The population of these colonies was about 250,000. Georgia, the 13th colony, was not settled until 1733.

The French, English, and Spanish influence in North America led to constant border wars, with some cities such as New York and Quebec moving from one colonizing power to another. Even Russia wrestled for colonial influence. In the 1600s Russia pushed from Siberia down the coastline of North America, disputing land rights with Spain along the way.

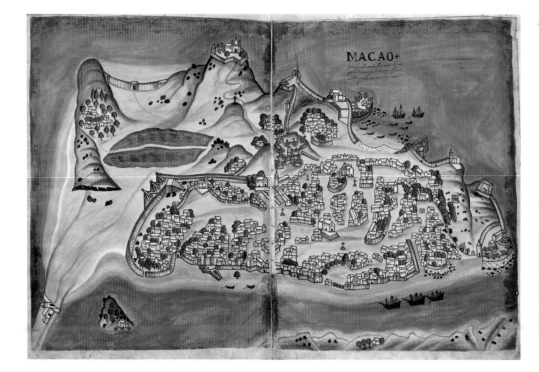

A map dating from 1646 of Macau, the Portuguese trading post on the coast of China.

SEE ALSO

- Aztec Empire
- Colonial wars
- Conquistadors
- Exploration
- Inca Empire
- Missionaries
- Spanish Empire
- Trade

COLUMBUS, CHRISTOPHER

Christopher Columbus (1451–1506) was one of history's most renowned mariners. In four voyages searching for a western sea route from Europe to Asia, he explored the Caribbean islands and the American mainland.

The son of a wool weaver, Columbus was born in Genoa, Italy, in 1451. At age 14 he went to sea. After several years as a sailor he moved to Lisbon, Portugal, then the center of seafaring and exploring in Europe. Columbus thought that it would be quicker to sail west to China, India, and the Indies rather than sailing east around Africa. In 1474 he began to search for a patron to fund his scheme. In April 1492 the Spanish Catholic monarchs Isabella of Castile and her husband Ferdinand of Aragon agreed to sponsor a voyage.

COLUMBUS'S VOYAGES

On August 3, 1492, Columbus navigated three ships, the *Santa Maria*, the *Pinta*, and the *Niña*, probably to Watling Island in the Bahamas, where he landed on October 12. Columbus believed that he had a god-given responsibility to spread Christianity in the new lands. He established a colony at Hispaniola, now Haiti and the Dominican Republic. He made three further voyages. On his third voyage Columbus reached the mainland of South America but was blamed for the breakdown in discipline in Hispaniola and returned to Spain in chains. Isabella eventually ordered his release and sponsored a fourth voyage, which ended in shipwreck in Jamaica. He returned to Spain and spent the rest of his life trying unsuccessfully to persuade Ferdinand and Isabella to fund another voyage. Although Columbus had become wealthy from his travels, he was disappointed that Spain did not acknowledge him enough. He died in Valladolid in 1506.

This portrait of the Genoese explorer Christopher Columbus was painted in 1519 after his death.

SEE ALSO

- Colonization
- Exploration
- Navigation
- Spain
- Spanish Empire

COMMUNICATIONS

In Europe communications improved dramatically over the 16th and 17th centuries. The rise of the printing press and the founding of national postal services led to information moving between people more efficiently.

At the beginning of the 16th century most people lived within the area where they were born. Roads were primitive and poorly maintained, making travel difficult. Most people occasionally went as far as the local town, and only a few might visit a city. There were few maps and limited knowledge of the wider world. Most people were illiterate, so news traveled by word of mouth. Rulers were among the few people who needed to communicate beyond their immediate surroundings in order to maintain order among their subjects. Couriers traveled on horses along dirt roads, carrying official letters and collecting replies. This system, inherited from the medieval period, evolved during the 1500s into a sophisticated network of collection and delivery points across Europe between which couriers and traders traveled.

ROYAL POSTAL SERVICES

In France King Louis XI had instituted in 1477 a royal postal service that employed 230 couriers. In 1516 King Henry VIII of England appointed a master of the post to maintain regular postal services along roads from London. Around 1510 the Hapsburg Emperor Maximilian I licensed a royal postal company to operate within the Holy Roman Empire. It was run by the Tassis family from Italy and was called the Thurn and Taxis postal service. At the height of its success in the late 17th century the Thurn and Taxis company employed 20,000 couriers, and the heads of the company were eventually made princes by Hapsburg rulers.

This Venetian 16th-century fresco by Italian artist Francesco Montemezzano shows a princess receiving a letter informing her of the progress of a distant battle.

Initial royal postal services across Europe were not available to the public, and the fees for transportation of mail were expensive. News traveled at the speed of the horse and could take many months to reach its destination.

BUSINESSES AND THE MAIL

During the 16th century Europe's rapidly expanding merchant class provided a catalyst for change. New entrepreneurs, or innovative businessmen, sought different ways to make their fortune. The publishing industry, for example, emerged after the invention of the printing press in the mid-15th century. At first, presses printed bibles, but soon they produced other books, including new translations of classical works. Increasing literacy and improvements in education prompted more people to read, and a broader market emerged for publishers. People increasingly demanded goods, such as books from around Europe, and it soon became clear that postal services could make businesses more efficient.

Companies therefore established their own postal services. In the early 17th century this coincided with a growing awareness among royal postal services that unofficial mail was being carried by royal couriers for illegal profit. Although postmasters were initially against this practice, it became evident that licensing royal couriers to carry private mail could be very profitable.

PUBLIC POSTAL SERVICES

A series of wars across Europe during the 16th century meant that communications became more important. For a while government postal services operated alongside private postal services. Governments eventually monopolized the mail, triggering a great leap forward for communications. In England in 1635 King Charles I made the royal mail available to the public with the cost of postage paid by the recipient. In France in 1672 postal services were made a state monopoly, and licenses were sold to private postal companies. The rest

A 17th-century woodcut showing a mounted postal courier in Westphalia, now part of Germany. He blows a horn to herald the arrival of new mail and to signify an opportunity for people to send letters.

THE BIRTH OF JOURNALISM

News pamphlets became popular in the 17th century partly because they contained news about foreign countries and gossip about people in authority. Kings, nobles, and politicians were all discussed. It was mainly for this reason that the writers and printers of the first newssheets preferred to remain anonymous. If criticism reached the royal court, royal agents were sent to search for the offending printer and his writers. If caught, they could be imprisoned. Some newssheets were sold very cheaply, but the sales were large, allowing the publishers to post free copies on walls as advertisements with a simple plea at the bottom: Supplico stet cedula (Please let the poster stand). Once a scandal or gossip reached the taverns, it was often immortalized in songs, which were then spread across the country by word of mouth. Many governments realized that direct force could not control the news industry and instead persuaded newspapers to obtain licenses. Once licensed, publishers were more easily controlled by taxation, censorship, and threats of legal prosecution.

of Europe followed over the next 100 years. The introduction of government mail services led to packages and letters being carried in bulk, quickly, and for lower set prices. Existing roads were improved, and new ones were built.

The first postal system in the American colonies was started in Massachusetts in 1639, when a tavern in Boston was designated as a repository for intracolony mail. Fast delivery arrived 150 years later with the first engineered roads. By 1672 there was an intercontinental mail service centered on New York. Mail was carried between America and Europe in 60 to 70 days.

THE POPULAR NEWS

Improved transportation made people increasingly curious about the outside world. Publishers and printing presses were quick to exploit the new market. Newspapers began as pamphlets (*see box*), which were distributed near the printers and carried farther by mail carriers. Most of the population was still illiterate, so the news reached people in different ways. The Venetian Senate held public readings of the news several times a day for a small fee. In countries such as England the news reached city and town dwellers by way of the town crier, an official who rang a bell and provided the time and news.

In an attempt to make newspapers accessible to more people, publishers started using common words that were more comprehensible to the poor reader. The actions of early publishers helped increase literacy, set standard grammar and spelling, and shape languages into recognizably modern forms.

A 17th-century engraving conveying the many roles of an early printer.

SEE ALSO

- Language
- Literacy
- Literature
- Maps and mapmaking
- Printing
- Trade
- Transportation

CONQUISTADORS

Conquistador is the Spanish word for "conqueror" and refers to soldiers who came from Spain to the Americas in the early 1500s, especially those who conquered Mexico and Peru. They achieved decisive victories over native peoples in the Americas and established the Spanish Empire.

The conquistadors' stated aims were to serve God and the Spanish king. They intended to convert native peoples to Christianity and to claim territory for the Spanish monarchs, who licensed their journeys. The motto on the campaign banner of the conquistador Hernán Cortés (1485–1547), for example, read: "Brothers and comrades, let us follow the sign of the cross in the true faith, for under this sign we shall conquer."

A portrait of the leading Spanish conquistador Hernán Cortés. Cortés took a small group of soldiers to Mexico in 1519. Within two years he had managed to conquer the powerful Aztec Empire of Mexico.

The conquistadors were also adventurers, however. Many were from poor regions of Spain, such as the dry inland province of Extremadura. They hoped to gain personal wealth and glory. Some fought more for any loot they could win than for the crown or Christianity. A contemporary chronicler described them as men "who come only until they can get some gold or wealth. They subordinate honor, morality, and honesty to this end, and commit innumerable crimes." Conquistadors amassed great fortunes and lands—Cortés governed most of Mexico, while Francisco Pizarro (about 1475–1541), who conquered the Incas of Peru, built a palace in his hometown of Trujillo—but they were also vital in the creation of the Spanish Empire.

CONQUEST OF MEXICO

Spanish sailors first landed on the Yucatán Peninsula, in modern Mexico, in 1517. They were attacked by local Mayans, but the survivors returned to the Spanish colony on Cuba with stories of gold, treasure, and great cities.

The stories reached Hernán Cortés, a nobleman from Extremadura who had moved to the Caribbean at age 19 to seek adventure. He had taken part in the Spanish conquest of Cuba, where he gained lands and a position in the government. Now Cortés prepared an expedition to Yucatán funded by the governor of Cuba, Diego Velazquez.

CONQVISTA DE MEXICO POR CORTES. N. 7

A 17th-century painting of the battle for the Aztec capital, Tenochtitlán. Under the leadership of Hernán Cortés Spanish forces overthrew the defending Aztecs. The Spanish horses were especially effective during the battle because they instilled fear in the Aztec warriors, who believed them to be gods.

Sensing that Cortés's independent spirit promised trouble, Velazquez tried to cancel the voyage. Cortés went ahead anyway. With 11 ships, about 600 men, and 16 horses he landed in Yucatán on March 4, 1519. He founded a settlement, Veracruz ("True Cross"), and declared himself in the service of the Spanish king.

ARRIVAL IN MEXICO

With the aid of a Spanish captive who had learned the Mayan language, Cortés began enlisting support from local peoples against the mighty Aztec Empire that dominated Mexico. Although outnumbered—600 soldiers faced an empire of millions—the Spanish had significant advantages. Their cannons and firearms were superior to native arrows and spears. Their horses had a great psychological effect on the Indians, who had never seen the animals before. Local peoples

were weakened by new diseases the Spanish unknowingly brought with them. Cortés was also aided by the myth of Quetzalcoatl, a god who would return from the east and free local peoples from tyranny. Representations of the god showed him as a white man with a beard, just as Cortés himself appeared. The conquistadors' greatest advantage, however, was that many local peoples resented their Aztec rulers, who took their crops and victims for sacrifice.

Combining diplomacy and force, Cortés subdued the peoples of the Yucatán, who gave him slaves and gold, and promised that greater wealth would come from the Aztec capital at Tenochtitlán (now Mexico City). Emissaries from the Aztec Emperor Montezuma gave Cortés gifts hoping to prevent an attack on the capital. Cortés moved inland toward Tenochtitlán, defeating or making alliances with cities along the way. Many swore loyalty to the Spanish out of fear or a desire to ally against the Aztecs on the winning side.

On arrival at the Aztec capital the conquistadors marveled at its size and beauty. Cortés was welcomed as an honored guest. A few months later, however, after Spanish soldiers had murdered 400 Atzec nobles, the city rose in revolt. Cortés and his men fought their way out of the city—Montezuma died in the fighting. Many Spaniards were killed or drowned in the city's canals, weighed down by the treasure they were carrying.

Cortés and his allies regrouped and marched again on the Aztec capital, where he arrived in May 1520. They besieged the city for three months, by which time three-quarters of it was destroyed, and its people were dying from wounds, smallpox, and hunger. Only two years after Cortés arrived in Mexico, Tenochtitlán, one of the world's greatest cities, surrendered to the Spanish in August 1521. With it fell the Aztec Empire.

CONQUEST OF THE INCAS

To the south, meanwhile, the mighty Inca Empire of the Andes Mountains of Peru again proved unable to resist a small band of Spaniards and the firearms and diseases they carried. The leader of the conquest was Francisco Pizarro, another adventurer from Extremadura. While exploring along the west coast of South America, Pizarro heard rumors of gold and silver mines in the region. Refused permission by the Spanish governor of Panama to explore further, he applied directly to King Charles I of Spain (ruled 1519–1556), who licensed Pizarro to explore and colonize the west coast of South America.

In many ways Pizarro's progress mirrored that of Cortés. As he marched toward the Inca capital Cuzco, he

A contemporary Aztec painting of Cortés (seated) negotiating with emissaries of the Aztec emperor Montezuma through his local interpreter, Doña Marina, who stands by his side. Doña Marina was an Aztec noble who had been given to Cortés as a slave. She helped Cortés establish friendly relations with the emperor and make allies on his journey to the Aztec capital.

found allies among the subject peoples of the empire. The Inca were weakened by civil war, and the people fell victim to diseases brought by the Spanish to which they had no resistance. The Inca emperor was one of the victims of smallpox.

Atahuallpa, the new Inca leader, fought Pizarro near Cuzco in 1532. Thousands of Inca soldiers met fewer than 200 Spaniards. Pizarro launched a cannon attack, and the Incas fled in panic. Around 1,500 Inca soldiers died; but there were no Spanish casualties, and Pizarro took Atahuallpa prisoner. The chief paid a huge ransom for his life—a room full of gold and silver—but Pizarro still had him executed. The Spanish then marched to Cuzco and put a puppet leader, Manco Capac, in power. In 1535 Pizarro founded Lima as the capital of Peru and began to organize the new territory. Tensions grew between Pizarro and his fellow conquistadors, who wanted more of a share of the loot. The struggle spilled over into violence, and Pizarro was killed by other Spaniards at his palace in Lima in 1541.

CONQUISTADORS' LEGACY

Although Cortés and Pizarro were the most famous of the conquistadors, they were not the only ones. Many of their companions also grew rich; some of them spent their wealth on luxurious homes or churches in the villages they came from in Spain. As Spanish power was consolidated in Central America, conquistadors continued to expand the borders of the Spanish Empire. Pedro de Alvarado, for example, whom Cortés sent south from Tenochtitlán, became governor of Guatemala.

The age of the conquistadors was comparatively brief—only about 30 years from the arrival of Cortés to the

conquest of Chile by one of the last conquistadors, Pedro de Valdivia, in the 1540s—but had huge consequences. Aided by firearms, luck, diplomacy, disease, and internal weakness, they had overthrown two mighty empires. They had changed the balance of the population of the Americas: When Cortés arrived in 1519, Mexico had around 25 million inhabitants. A century later the figure had dropped to around one million, mainly due to European diseases.

The conquistadors had opened the way for Spain to build its American empire. As their generation passed, the civil servants, priests, and settlers who took their place would be a very different sort of person. Although their priorities were long-term development and settlement rather than instant exploitation, they remained as interested as their forerunners in the wealth of the "New World."

A contemporary engraving of conquistador Francisco Pizarro, ordering the death of his treacherous partner Almagro. A dispute over control of the Inca capital Cuzco led to Almagro's death.

SEE ALSO

- Aztec Empire
- Columbus, Christopher
- Diplomacy
- Exploration
- Inca Empire
- Latin America
- Spain
- Spanish Empire

CONTINUITY AND CHANGE

The period 1500 to 1700 marked a transition between the Medieval and Modern worlds when Europeans extended their influence around the globe. Although dramatic changes took place during this era, in some ways life continued much as it had for centuries.

For most Europeans throughout this period life continued to be linked to agriculture. Most jobs were connected with farming either directly or indirectly, as in trades such as brewing or cloth production. Most people still lived in the countryside—in 1600 only around 5 percent of people lived in cities—and few traveled farther than the nearest town or market in their lives. The working day still began at dawn and ended at dusk. The standard diet remained based on vegetables and cereals such as wheat, occasionally supplemented with meat.

TIME OF CHANGE

Even against the unchanging rhythms of the agricultural cycle, however, the pace of life began to alter. From the 14th century town clocks began to strike every hour, imposing new divisions on the day. In the 16th century technological breakthroughs made clocks smaller and more accurate, and more common. As European maritime exploration matured, the European diet changed. At first only the rich benefited, because only they could afford spices from the East Indies to improve the taste of flavorless or bad meat. Later, however, the introduction of new staple foods such as corn and potatoes from the Americas began to change the diet even of poorer people across the continent.

RELIGIOUS CHANGE

Europe remained nearly entirely Christian, although some countries had small populations of Jews and Muslims. Faith and worship were at the center of

A 16th-century painting of a caravel. Improvements in sailing ships allowed Europeans to establish trade routes around the world.

existence. Christianity underwent great change, however, with the Protestant Reformation of the 16th century.

The reformers such as Martin Luther and John Calvin believed that the church had become corrupt. They aimed to return to the purity of the early Christian church, stripping away all traditions and practices not found in the Bible. They believed the Bible, not the church, to be the ultimate spiritual authority. The impulse given to the reformed Protestant churches was matched by a reinvigoration of the Catholic church.

Protestants stressed the importance of reading the Bible for oneself. That development in turn was only made possible by the spread of printing technology, which allowed books to be produced much more cheaply. The growing number of books both encouraged and depended on a parallel growth in literacy (the ability to read)

A 17th-century engraving showing a printer's workshop in Germany. The development of printing from the mid-15th century led to an explosion in the spread of new ideas in religion and science, and encouraged an increase in literacy.

and an emphasis on books in local languages rather than Latin, the common language of scholarship and religion. In 1500 Europe was a largely illiterate continent; by 1700 countries such as England, the Netherlands, and the Italian city-states had literacy rates as high as 80 percent, although rates tended to be lower in the countryside.

Although no state introduced public education for all of its citizens, the number of schools and tutors for the middle and upper classes grew. So too did the number of universities where students learned medicine, theology, or law. The universities were important to provide a steady supply of clerks, notaries, and secretaries to work for national governments.

THE NEW SHAPE OF EUROPE

The 16th and 17th centuries marked the emergence of modern nation-states. Most notably in France monarchs

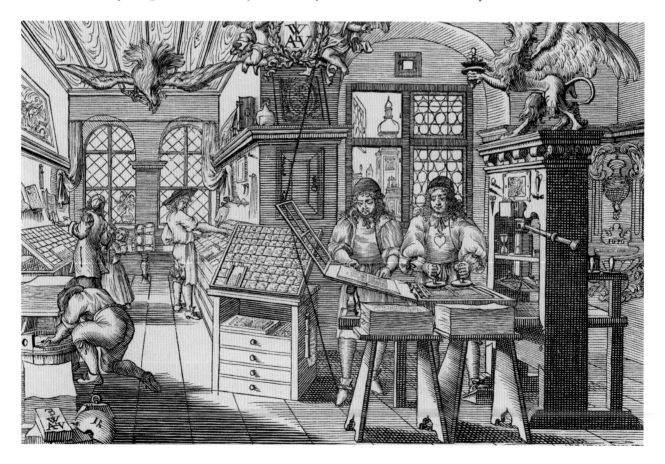

established apparatus to keep central records, collect taxes, and organize the military. As states built palaces, parliaments, and government offices, capital cities such as Paris and London grew in size and importance.

RELIGIOUS INTOLERANCE

In Italy and Spain religious courts known as inquisitions had been rooting out heresy (beliefs that differed from those of the church) for centuries. The spread of Reformation ideas and new scientific discoveries led the inquisitions to intensify their efforts to enforce uniform beliefs. Meanwhile, Protestant states were zealous in their persecution of Catholics. Both faiths turned on those accused of witchcraft. During this period many thousands of people were burned as witches.

Partly as a consequence of religious intolerance and the strife it caused, life for many Europeans remained short and often brutal. The Thirty Years' War (1618–1648), a long series of conflicts between Catholic and Protestant rulers, killed at least 10 to 15 percent of civilians in parts of modern Germany, where it was fought. Most casualties were caused by hunger after fighting ruined the harvests. Other conflicts and civil wars claimed many lives in the Netherlands, France, and England.

HARSH LIVES

Life expectancy was short, even among the rich. In the English aristocracy in the 17th century, for example, it was around 32 years for men and 35 years for women. The death rate for children was very high: 20 to 25 percent died before age four. Epidemics of plague or influenza killed millions of people. The inability of governments to cope with poor harvests meant that even at the end of the 17th century Europeans still died of hunger.

While many aspects of the lives of Europeans in 1700 would have been familiar to their forebears of 1500, more profound changes were also taking place. Trade networks had linked Europe with Asia since ancient times, but now European mariners found new sea routes to India and East Asia.

Christopher Columbus's arrival in the Americas in 1492 began a long process of colonization and change. The event was a disaster for many native peoples, who were almost wiped out by European diseases to which they had no resistance. In addition, this period marked the beginning of the African slave trade in which thousands of people were imported from Africa to work as slaves in the Americas.

In Europe, meanwhile, gold and silver from the Americas, together with raw materials such as coffee, sugar, and cotton, contributed to the economic growth that would fund the continent's expansion to become a global power.

A painting of the cathedral and market place in Aachen, Germany, in the 16th century. As more people moved to towns and cities, they were drawn into a money-based economy.

SEE ALSO

- Calvin, John
- Catholic church
- Colonization
- Council of Trent
- Exploration
- Luther, Martin
- Trade

COPERNICUS, NICOLAUS

Polish astronomer Nicolaus Copernicus (1473–1543) is famous for his heliocentric, or "sun-centered," theory for the universe. He argued, against contemporary beliefs, that the sun is at the center of the planetary system, and earth revolves around it.

The son of a merchant, Mikolaj Kopernik, who was later known by his Latinized pen name Nicolaus Copernicus, was born in 1473 in the town of Torun in Poland. When he was 10 years old, his father died, so Nicolaus and his brother Andreas were brought up by their uncle, a bishop in the Catholic church. Copernicus enjoyed an excellent education. He studied mathematics, medicine, and philosophy at the University of Cracow. He then traveled to Italy, where he studied law at Bologna and medicine at Padua, and lectured in Rome. In 1512 he took up residence as a canon, or church official, of Frauenburg cathedral in East Prussia, a position he held for the rest of his life. There he scrutinized the night sky from one of his rooms, which he made into an observatory.

COPERNICUS'S EARLY WORK

Over the following years Copernicus formulated ideas on the structure of the universe. He explained them in a book known as the *Commentariolus*, which was later expanded into his

major work *De Revolutionibus Orbium Coelestium*, (Concerning the Revolutions of the Heavenly Orbs). He only circulated his work among close friends at first because he feared its content might cause uproar in the religious and scientific communities. In the *Commentariolus* Copernicus argued that the earth is not the center of the universe, that the rotation of the earth accounts for the apparent rotation of the stars, that the annual cycle of the

A drawing from 1873 made from an earlier portrait of Nicolaus Copernicus. He is shown holding instruments with which he charted the movements of the planets.

sun is caused by the earth revolving around it, and that the earth turns once daily on its axis. Copernicus's studies revolutionized the traditional geocentric, or "earth-centered," view of the universe.

THE PTOLEMAIC UNIVERSE

The view of the universe that dominated medieval thinking was known as Ptolemaic for Ptolemy, a second-century A.D. astronomer from Alexandria, Egypt. According to Ptolemy, the earth was stationary at the center of the universe. Around the earth revolved the sun and the planets, which were attached to moving concentric spheres. These planet-bearing spheres were transparent and moved in perfect circles at a constant speed. Only the outermost sphere did not move; it held what were known as the "fixed stars." One problem that Ptolemy had to contend with was that some of the planets occasionally appeared to move backward in the sky. To account for this, Ptolemy suggested that the planets also made orbits around smaller circles known as epicycles.

THE SUN-CENTERED UNIVERSE

Copernicus believed it was unlikely that a large body like the sun would orbit a small body such as the earth. He proposed that the earth revolves around the sun during the course of a year, and that it rotates on its axis during a day. He did not reject all of Ptolemy's system, however. For example, he supported Ptolemy's idea that the planets moved at a constant speed in perfect circular orbits. Astronomers know that planets in fact follow eliptical (oval) orbits.

Copernicus completed the text of *De Revolutionibus* by about 1530. He decided not to publish it then, perhaps

because he feared its reception by the church, but more likely because he did not want to be ridiculed for challenging common sense. For centuries Christians had assumed that the earth, God's creation, was at the center of the universe. Humans, whom God had made in his image, stood at the center of his creation and were masters of nature. People in the 16th century believed that any theory putting the earth at the center of the universe diminished the status of humankind.

De Revolutionibus was eventually printed in 1543, the year Copernicus died. Legend has it that Copernicus was handed an early copy of his book on his deathbed and managed to read it before he died. Although it took many years before the impact of the work was widely felt, Copernicus is now acknowledged as having freed astronomy from its geocentric point of view. His work made an important contribution to later discoveries in astronomy by scientists such as Galileo Galilei (1564–1642).

A representation dating from 1660 of Copernicus's heliocentric (sun-centered) universe. The earth in its four seasons is shown following its orbit around the sun.

SEE ALSO

- Astronomy
- Clocks and calendars
- Galileo Galilei
- Inventions and inventors
- Newton, Isaac
- Science

COUNCIL OF TRENT

As the Catholic church responded to the Reformation in the mid-16th century, a church council met at the city of Trent in northern Italy to reaffirm church doctrines, correct abuses within the church, and counter Protestant challenges to the church hierarchy.

The aim of the Council of Trent was to clarify the position of the Catholic church following Protestant calls for reform. The council sessions were lengthy and complex because different factions wanted different outcomes. While some of the participants wanted to return Protestants to the Catholic faith, for example, others preferred to let the division between the churches stand. Politics was also involved. The French King Francis I was worried that the council might favor his political rival, Charles V, the Holy Roman emperor. In addition, successive popes were concerned that the council would strengthen conciliarism, the idea that church councils should have more authority than the papacy.

THE COUNCIL BEGINS
The Council of Trent met three times over a period of nearly 20 years but spent only four and a half years in session. The first session met from 1545 to 1547, after Charles V and Francis I agreed to urge Pope Paul III to establish the council. Charles was motivated by the idea that Protestants would return to the Catholic church if enough effort was made to correct clerical abuses. The council's delegates

were bishops and other clerical authorities who came mostly from Italy, Spain, Germany, and France. The number of delegates in attendance varied from 35 to 250.

A painting of the third session of the Council of Trent (1562–1563).

The first meeting of the council came to important decisions that emphasized the differences between Catholicism and the reformed religions. For example, while Protestants believed that Christianity should be founded solely on the authority of the Bible, the council affirmed that the traditional wisdom of the church carried equal authority with the holy scriptures. While Protestants supported new translations of the Bible into German, English, and other languages, the council stated that the only authoritative text was the Latin Vulgate version. The delegates confirmed the status of the traditional seven sacraments, or acts regarded as outward signs of inward grace. They were baptism, confirmation, the Eucharist (ritually eating food and drinking wine said to be Christ's flesh and blood), penance, unction (anointing the sick), holy orders (being ordained), and marriage. Protestants acknowledged only baptism and the Eucharist.

Luther's central idea of "justification by faith" was a great obstacle to reconciliation between the Catholic church and Protestants. Luther believed that the only requirement for a Christian to be saved from sin was faith in God. The council reasserted that while faith was indeed necessary for

REFORMING POPE

Born in 1468, Alessandro Farnese, who later became Pope Paul III, was educated in Florence and Rome. Soon he became cardinal deacon, bishop of Parma and of Ostia, and dean of the Sacred College (the cardinals of the church). In 1534 he was elected pope and set about revitalizing the city of Rome by encouraging agriculture and municipal building projects. He enlarged the Vatican library, made important academic appointments at the University of Rome, and commissioned Michelangelo to paint *The Last Judgment* on the wall of the Vatican's Sistine Chapel.

Paul III appointed new cardinals renowned for their integrity and set up a commission to report on the state of the church. In 1537 it delivered a damning assessment of the church's faults, but Paul did not immediately enforce any great changes within the church hierarchy. In 1540 he formally approved the founding of the Jesuit order, and two years later he established the Inquisition in Rome to enforce discipline among Catholics and to eradicate heresy. In 1545 he convened the Council of Trent.

Paul III was typical of the Renaissance popes whose worldly behavior was condemned by Protestants and Catholics alike. He fathered four children, gave his relatives jobs in the church, and enjoyed the pleasures of life. Yet he was also committed to reform within the church and worked hard to ensure that the Council of Trent took place.

A portrait of Pope Paul III painted around 1543 by Italian Renaissance artist Titian (about 1490–1576).

salvation, performing good works and participating in the sacraments also helped people reach salvation.

As well as clarifying doctrines, the first meeting of the council also addressed the problem of clerical abuses within the church. It decreed that bishops and priests had to preach on a regular basis, and bishops should live in their dioceses or whatever area they are responsible for. The council also condemned pluralism, in which a churchman held more than one post and collected more than one income.

THE SECOND MEETING

Charles V instigated the second meeting of the council, hoping finally to unify his embattled empire under the Catholic church. It lasted from 1551 to 1552, and Charles invited a number of Protestant observers. One of the most significant doctrines discussed was transubstantiation. The church traditionally believed that when a priest consecrated the bread and wine used during the Eucharist, or Mass, they literally became the body and blood of Christ. The reformers objected that the presence of Christ in the bread and wine was symbolic, not literal. The council affirmed the traditional teaching. It also affirmed the spiritual value of pilgrimages and penances rejected by Protestants.

REACHING A CONCLUSION

The third and final meeting of the council took place from 1562 to 1563. It revolved around the power struggle between the representatives of the pope and champions of the interests of France, Spain, and the Holy Roman emperor. At the end of the session the pope's supporters prevailed.

The delegates to the Council of Trent agreed to uphold certain principles. Clergy were to be celibate,

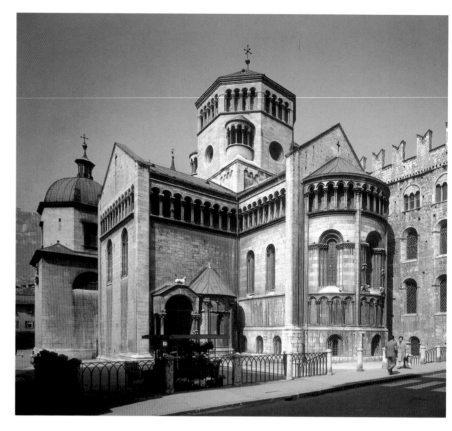

and during Mass lay people could receive only the bread but not the wine, both points disputed by Protestants. Bishops were ordered to establish seminaries, or training colleges, for priests in their dioceses. In addition, the council declared that holy relics and images could be venerated.

The council eventually ended on December 4, 1563. The decisions made by the council were conservative. They disappointed those Catholics who had hoped for more dramatic reform. The pope retained his supreme position at the head of the church, and most traditional doctrines were endorsed. Although the process clarified Catholic teachings, it alienated Protestants. It had a profound effect on clerical discipline, making bishops and priests more responsible and dedicated churchmen. This in turn improved morale within the church and helped reestablish and revitalize Catholicism in many parts of Europe.

A modern view of the cathedral in Trent, in northern Italy. It dates from the 12th century and was built in the Romanesque style. European representatives of the Catholic church met inside the cathedral during the sessions of the Council of Trent between 1545 and 1563.

SEE ALSO
• Catholic church
• Counter Reformation
• Papacy
• Reformation

COUNTER REFORMATION

The Counter Reformation, or Catholic Reformation, is the name given to the Catholic church's response to the Protestant Reformation during the 16th and early 17th centuries. Its many aspects included spiritual renewal, religious repression, and cultural expression.

The Reformation began in 1517, when Martin Luther, a German monk, called for reforms within the Catholic church. Many in the Catholic church agreed with the need for reform to counter abuses. Unlike Luther and the other Protestant reformers who broke away and set up new churches, others sought changes within the Catholic church. The Counter Reformation was the church hierarchy's response to the growing pressure for reform.

The church had been undergoing a spiritual revival since the late 15th century. In Italy and Spain Catholics dissatisfied with the worldliness of the church created new religious orders or

The Triumph of the Church (about 1628) by Peter Paul Rubens shows the Virgin Mary in a golden chariot to symbolize the resurgence of the Catholic church.

JOHN OF THE CROSS

John of the Cross was one of the most important spiritual teachers during the Counter Reformation. He was born in 1542 near Avila in Spain. He studied at a Jesuit college in Medina, then joined the Carmelite order in 1563. In 1567 he was ordained a priest, and in the same year he met Teresa of Avila. They embarked on a mission to reform the Carmelite order. In 1568 John and two other Carmelite friars established a reformed house in the town of Duruelo, the first of 15 he founded. Some of his fellow Carmelites resented the proposed changes, and in 1577 some of them imprisoned him in Toledo, where he was kept in a tiny windowless cell. Eventually he escaped and continued to work on the spiritual writings he had started during captivity. In them he talked about what he called the "dark night of the soul," a period of spiritual suffering on his inward journey to God. For the rest of his life John gave spiritual guidance and wrote his influential works, which included some of the finest examples of Spanish poetry. He died in 1591. He was made a saint in 1726.

A 17th-century portrait of John of the Cross, a reforming priest in an order of the Catholic church called the Carmelites.

reformed existing orders to emphasize stricter forms of piety and devotion. The Franciscans, for example, took vows of poverty and lived by begging. In Italy the Capuchins—named for their pointed hood, or *cappuchio*—lived austere lives, tending the sick and preaching among their communities.

NEW ORDERS

After Luther's protest launched the Reformation, new religious orders continued to emerge. They included the Theatines in Rome and the Barnabites. In the 1560s two Spanish Carmelites, Teresa of Avila and John of the Cross (*see box*), effectively created a new order. The Discalced ("Barefoot") Carmelites got their name because their members wore sandals rather than shoes to demonstrate their humility.

The most influential and dynamic of the new orders were the Jesuits, or Society of Jesus. Founded by a former Spanish soldier named Ignatius Loyola (1491–1556), the Jesuits were approved in 1540 by Pope Paul III (pope 1534–1549). Loyola organized the Jesuits like an army, commanded by himself and his priests, and notable for their discipline, learning, spiritual fervor, and loyalty to the pope. The Jesuits emphasized education, founding many schools. They also shared with other orders a commitment to missionary work both in non-Catholic parts of Europe and around the world.

THE COUNCIL OF TRENT

Despite the reform of religious orders, the Protestant Reformation itself initially provoked little formal reaction from the church leadership. In 1545, however, Pope Paul III convened a church council in the Italian city of Trent to clarify church doctrine and implement reforms. The Council of Trent met in three major sessions

The nave or central hall and the choir of Santo Domingo in Oaxaca, Mexico. The church was built in the 17th century by Dominican priests. While the Catholic church lost supporters in Europe as a result of the Reformation, it gained many followers in the Americas and Asia.

between 1545 and 1563. Some of the council's resolutions recognized the need for reform within the church, such as the need for better training for the clergy. Many council decisions, however, particularly regarding doctrine, were deeply conservative.

COUNCIL DECISIONS

The council rejected the Protestant emphasis on the Bible as the sole source of religious authority; it reasserted that the traditional wisdom of the church had equal weight. In the face of Protestant determination to make the Bible more accessible by translating it into local languages, the council reaffirmed the Latin Vulgate Bible as the only authorized version. The council also asserted the traditional hierarchy of the clergy, headed by the pope. It reaffirmed aspects of worship to which Protestants objected, including the celebration of seven sacraments (Protestants observed only

REPRESSIVE MEASURES

The Catholic reform movement included repressive measures such as the Inquisition. This religious court had been established in the 13th century to prosecute heretics (people whose beliefs differed from those of the church). At the end of the 15th century the Spanish monarchs founded an Inquisition to support their reunification of Spain. Notorious for its use of torture, the Spanish Inquisition later turned its attention to Protestants, although it was condemned for being overzealous. In 1542 Pope Paul III founded another version of the Inquisition in Rome, which was officially known as the Holy Office and operated mainly in Italy. One of its victims was the astronomer Galileo Galilei (1564–1642), who in 1633 was accused of heretical teachings and sentenced to house arrest for the rest of his life.

The Index of Prohibited Books was another means of combatting heresy and instilling discipline. First issued in 1559 by a section of the Roman Inquisition, the Index was a list of books that were condemned as either heretical or damaging to faith or morals. Catholics were forbidden to read books on the list. One of the best-known books on the Index was *De Revolutionibus* by the astronomer Nicolaus Copernicus (1473–1543). It was not removed from the list until 1757.

two), the holiness of religious relics such as the bones of saints, and the effectiveness of making pilgrimages.

EXPANDING THE CHURCH

One of the most dynamic expressions of the reinvigorated Catholic faith during the Counter Reformation was the emphasis on missionary work. Highly able priests, monks, and nuns dedicated themselves to spreading the faith both in Europe and overseas.

In Europe they tried to reconvert followers in countries that had adopted Protestantism, such as England, Germany, and the Netherlands. Such a course of action could be dangerous. After joining the Jesuits in Rome in 1573, Edmund Campion led the first Jesuit mission to England in 1580. He preached in London and northern England, and published a pamphlet defending Catholicism. The alarmed government of the Protestant Queen Elizabeth I tried Campion for treason; he was found guilty, tortured, and executed in 1581.

Jesuits, along with the Dominicans, Franciscans, and Augustinians, traveled to the Americas, India, and East Asia in search of converts. One outstanding example of an overseas missionary was Francis Xavier (1506–1552), one of the first Jesuits. Xavier worked for seven years at the Portuguese colony of Goa and for two more in Japan. When he died in 1552, he was on his way to continue his mission in China.

In 1622 Pope Gregory XV founded the Congregation for the Propagation of the Faith to coordinate missions inside and outside France. In 1663 French Catholics began the Foreign Missionary Society of Paris, which was set up to encourage missionary work in Southeast Asia.

FRANCIS DE SALES (1567–1622)

One of the leading figures of the Counter Reformation, Francis de Sales converted Protestants and became known as an inspirational spiritual teacher. Francis was born in 1567 in Savoy, a small duchy on the borders of modern France and Italy. Educated by Jesuits in Paris, he studied law at Padua in Italy before entering the church. In 1593 he began his mission to convert the Calvinists of Chablais, a region on the southern side of Lake Geneva. Although he encountered hostility, he impressed people with his integrity and piety. In 1602 he was appointed bishop of Geneva, and later, together with Jane Frances of Chantal, he founded the Visitation of Holy Mary, a religious order for women who were not suited to the harsher regimes of some traditional orders. Francis was also a writer, and his *Introduction to the Devout Life* became a spiritual classic. He died in 1622 while visiting Lyons, France.

A 17th-century portrait of Francis de Sales, a famous preacher of Counter Reformation ideas in France.

Although the Counter Reformation was a largely religious response to the Reformation, it also had a political dimension. In Spain, Italy, and the Holy Roman Empire, which included modern Germany and parts of Central Europe, Catholic monarchs supported the church to reinforce their own power. Their opponents often promoted Protestantism in their turn.

POLITICAL SUPPORT

Holy Roman Emperor Charles V (1500–1558) strongly supported the Catholic church's attempts to reform, since the Protestant movement was particularly successful in the states of the Holy Roman Empire. Charles fought several wars against the Protestants but eventually agreed to the Peace of Augsburg in 1555. The agreement recognized Lutheran Protestants and determined that the religion of a state in the empire would be that of its ruler. Charles intended this to be a temporary compromise. The following decades saw the Counter Reformation being implemented across Germany in an effort to win people back to Catholicism.

Holy Roman Emperor Ferdinand II (1578–1637) was also a champion of the Counter Reformation. Many nobles in lands under his rule—Austria, Hungary, and Bohemia—were Protestant. By enforcing Catholicism, Ferdinand bolstered his own power. However, the Bohemian nobles revolted against Ferdinand, sparking the Thirty Years' War (1618–1648). It was a prolonged series of conflicts among European powers that had a mixture of political and religious causes. The war finally ended in 1648 with the Treaty of Westphalia, which is sometimes taken as the effective end

The facade of Saint Peter's basilica in Rome, completed between 1607 and 1614 by architect Carlo Maderna, was a striking demonstration of the vigor of the Catholic church during the Counter Reformation.

of the Counter Reformation. However, many of the currents of change in the church continued later.

The Treaty of Westphalia reaffirmed the Augsburg principle of allowing rulers to choose the state religion and extended it to include Calvinists. States were deemed to be Catholic or Protestant according to their situation in 1624. If a ruler later changed religion, that would not affect the religion of the state. This effectively brought to an end further spread of both the Reformation and Counter Reformation in Europe.

ART AND SPIRITUALITY

The Counter Reformation was marked by a fresh impetus and spirituality in artistic expression. The new facade built for Saint Peter's basilica in Rome, the most important of all Catholic churches, summed up the triumphant confidence of the faith. Elsewhere church architecture placed an emphasis on grandeur, with ornate decoration and rich gold and silver gilt.

In music the Italian composer Palestrina (about 1525–1594) reflected the spirit of the Council of Trent with sacred polyphonic ("many-voiced") compositions that displayed rich harmonies despite their underlying conservatism. In painting there was a new emphasis on realism and the depiction of emotion in images of Christ on the cross or the martyrdom of the saints. Leading Counter Reformation artists included El Greco in Spain (1541–1614), Peter Paul Rubens (1577–1640) in the Spanish Netherlands, and Gian Lorenzo Bernini (1598–1680) in Italy.

By the time the energy of the Counter Reformation faded in the

This crucifix was made from silver and precious stones in around 1530. While Protestant faiths emphasized simplicity in architecture and religious art, the Catholic church used ornate architecture and artworks to glorify its faith.

mid-17th century, internal reform, discipline, political support, and missionary work had revitalized the Catholic church. The church had reassserted its doctrines and largely recovered its stability after decades of Protestant inroads. Catholicism had also reclaimed southern Germany, Austria, and other parts of Europe, as well as winning around three million converts in the Americas and Asia.

SEE ALSO

- Baroque
- Bernini, Gian Lorenzo
- Catholic church
- Clergy
- Council of Trent
- Jesuits
- Missionaries
- Music
- Papacy
- Teresa of Avila

COURTS AND COURTIERS

At the start of the Reformation many courts were centers of local power and patronage. By the end of the 17th century the rise of absolute monarchs had made the prestige of a court essential to the power of the state. Complex rules governed the behavior of courtiers.

As rulers emerged in states across Europe thanks to wealth or warfare, they developed a courtly life designed to reinforce their position as head of the political and social hierarchy. Rulers' hold on power was sometimes weak and often open to challenge by violence. Their courtiers were often other aristocrats or social leaders who could provide protection and help run the state. Sometimes they were little more than bodyguards or gangs. By taking such powerful figures into their courts, rulers tried to prevent a challenge to their own power. By commissioning leading artists,

A painting of a procession in which courtiers carry Queen Elizabeth I through London. She used her image at court to reinforce her power.

A portrait of the Italian poet Torquato Tasso (1544–1595) who spent many years at the brilliant court of the Este family in Ferrara. He found life at court difficult and had a mental breakdown. He spent his last years wandering from court to court looking for the ideal conditions in which to work.

composers, writers, and scholars, they also created an impression of splendor and religious devotion to help increase their own prestige and legitimacy. In doing so, they created dynamic cultural centers of the Renaissance.

Perhaps the most influential of the Renaissance courts was that of the dukes of Burgundy, whose lands lay in eastern France and the Netherlands. In the 14th and 15th centuries the Burgundian dukes were great patrons of the arts, especially music. They ruled over the most extravagant and cultured court in Europe.

Other leading Renaissance courts were found in the Italian city-states, such as that of the Este family at Ferrara and those of the Sforza at Milan, the Gonzaga at Mantua, and the Montefeltro family at Urbino. The last provided the model court in the influential Book *The Courtier* (1528) by Baldassare Castiglione (*see box*).

ENGLAND'S MONARCHY

The Courtier was translated into several languages and became highly influential in other European courts. In England the Tudor family had reigned since their victory in the Wars of the Roses in 1485. Again, the monarchs' courtiers were aristocrats and their families. The more time they spent at court in London, or at any of the more temporary locations of the court, the less time they had to raise their own local power bases from which they might challenge Tudor authority. The Tudors, meanwhile, ran their government through a series of highly capable ministers or administrators.

In the reigns of Henry VIII (ruled 1509–1547) and his daughter Elizabeth I (ruled 1558–1603) English courtly life evolved into a conspicuous and tightly controlled display of wealth and position. The Tudors commissioned artists to paint portraits that projected an image of power to their subjects. During Elizabeth's reign English poets and artists developed a cult of the "virgin queen" idolizing the monarch's purity and dedication to her country.

THE COURTIER

In *The Courtier* Baldassare Castiglione sets out to describe the essential characteristics of the perfect courtier. As a youth, Castiglione enjoyed life at Ludovico Sforza's court in Milan. He then served the Gonzaga and Montefeltro rulers, and also carried out diplomatic missions in Spain and England.

Castiglione's ideas about the ideal courtier are expressed in a series of imaginary conversations at the court of Urbino. Castiglione portrays the courtier as the *uomo universale*, the universal man. In addition to noble birth the courtier must possess good looks and demonstrate bravery. The courtier must also be skilled in military arts, sports, dancing and languages. He has to be well-read and have a taste for art and music. The hallmark ability of Castiglione's courtier was *sprezzatura*, or an air of effortless achievement. The combination of breeding and education was hoped to produce an individual who could help create the perfect state.

Preserving the image required a strict system of hierarchy and behavior. Courtiers were still usually local nobles who could provide or lead troops on the monarch's behalf or perform other duties such as diplomatic missions. Those who pleased the monarch were rewarded with titles and land; those who did not were punished, sometimes even with death.

A NEW STYLE OF RULER

In the first half of the 17th century the French court was the setting for the development of a new idea of ruling known as absolutism, in which a king or queen exercised sole power by "divine right." The monarch was obliged, however, to exercise power for the good of his or her subjects. With the new ideas came a new type of court and a new role for the courtier. Louis XIII (ruled 1610–1643) reduced the power of the nobility and strengthened that of the monarchy, which had been weakened during the bitter religious wars of the 16th century.

Louis's successor, Louis XIV (ruled 1643–1715), brought absolute monarchy to its height. He built a palace at Versailles, near Paris, to underline his power. The palace was spectacular, its gardens highly formal, and its furnishings luxurious for the time. Even at Versailles, however, rooms grew so cold in winter wine could freeze in glasses during dinner. The palace was full of paintings and sculptures of Louis himself in heroic poses and in the guise of the "Sun King" on whom France depended.

THE COURT AT VERSAILLES

At Versailles Louis could watch his nobles carefully. By controlling political favor through the court, he made sure that they had to live at Versailles if they wished to prosper. Of the 20,000 people attached to the court, around 1,000 nobles lived in the palace itself, together with around 4,000 servants. Life at Versailles was a long round of etiquette punctuated by extravagant rituals designed to reinforce the king's position. A culture developed in which manners and refinement were more important to a courtier than a practical achievement such as military prowess.

Courtiers were expected to keep their feelings under control and to

A 17th-century painting of the French philosopher René Descartes at Queen Christina's court in Sweden. There he taught the monarch his Cartesian form of philosophy.

dedicate themselves to the well-being of the state in the person of the king. The corridors of Versailles became notorious for petty squabbles, sexual scandal, and political intrigues.

Versailles set the model for royal residences throughout Europe as absolute monarchies emerged in Spain, Portugal, Austria, and Prussia. The monarchs created glittering courts that served to reduce the power of the formerly independent nobility. Now noble courtiers depended entirely on the monarch and his or her favor.

SEE ALSO

- Drama
- Elizabeth I
- Italian states
- Louis XIV
- Poetry
- Renaissance
- Versailles

CRIME AND PUNISHMENT

Throughout the 16th and 17th centuries criminals habitually received punishments that we would today consider harsh. Minor crimes were often punished by public display. Other crimes earned the death penalty, which was applied in different ways according to the nature of the crime.

There were few law enforcement officers in the 16th and 17th centuries, so most areas had to police themselves. As a result, many crimes went unprosecuted and unpunished, making it difficult to accurately assess crime levels.

Social and economic changes in the 16th century led to an increasing number of vagabonds, beggars, and other people living on the edge of society. They included landless and unemployed peasants, ex-soldiers, and immigrants. Such people moved from village to village in search of work and were often blamed for any crimes committed in an area.

URBAN CRIME

Many outcasts gravitated toward towns, where they joined the lowest level of society. Poor urban living conditions encouraged crime, and organized gangs of thieves operated in most European towns and cities. Different gangs specialized in different crimes, such as picking pockets or robbing shops. The criminal underworld had its own language, rules, and customs.

In England London's criminal subculture included highway robbers. These men lay in wait for their victims on deserted country roads around the

capital. They held up travelers, often at gunpoint, and stole their cash and jewelry. They were known as highwaymen, and their activities captured the public imagination. Because they robbed on horseback, they were considered "gentlemanly."

A set of 16th-century stocks. Criminals' hands and feet were held between wooden planks for the term of their sentence.

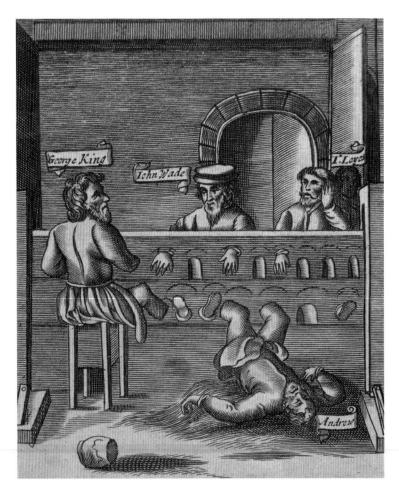

A public hanging at Tyburn, London, in 1696. The gallows known as the "triple tree" was erected in 1571, allowing several people to be hanged at once. Public executions took place four times a year and attracted crowds of spectators.

There were many stories about the bravery and gallant behavior of highwaymen such as Claude Duvall (executed in 1670).

Few convicted highwaymen were in fact gentlemen. When the upper classes committed crimes like murder, robbery, and extortion, they were often able to avoid punishment under the justice system of the time by using their influence and money to bribe judges.

TYPES OF PUNISHMENT

Punishments were extremely harsh. For example, in England in the reign of Henry VIII (ruled 1509–1547) 700 types of crime merited the death penalty. More than 72,000 felons were hanged in the period.

Punishments for minor offenses ranged from whipping or branding to exposure in the stocks or the pillory. Such punishments were designed to shame a wrongdoer. The stocks and pillory were hinged wooden boards

A CONDEMNED MAN

In England a person condemned to be hanged usually gave a last speech on the gallows, confessing his or her sins. These speeches were often published and were very popular with the crowds. This is an extract from the dying speech of the pickpocket John Selman, hanged at Charing Cross, London, on January 7, 1612.

"I am come patiently to offer up the sweet, and dear sacrifice of my life, a life which I have gracelessly abused, and by the unruly course thereof, made my death a scandal to my kindred and acquaintance: I have consumed fortune's gifts in riotous companies, wasted my good name in the purchase of goods unlawfully gotten, and now ending my days in too late repentance, I am placed in the rank of reprobates, which the rusty canker of time must needs turn to oblivion. I stand here as shame's example, ready to be spewed out of the Commonwealth.

"I confess, I have known too much, performed more, but consented to most: I have been the only corruption of many ripe witted youth, and leader of them to confusion. Pardon me God, for that is now a burden to my conscience, wash it away sweet Creator, that I may spotless enter into thy glorious kingdom."

A 16th-century engraving of the execution of the Amboise conspirators. In 1560 Protestant members of the lesser French nobility tried to overthrow the Catholic king of France, Francis II, but they were caught. They were convicted of treason and later sentenced to public execution by hanging and beheading.

with holes in them. In the stocks people's hands and feet were held, while in the pillory a person's head and hands were. Criminals would be locked in for a specified period depending on the crime. They were then humiliated by people throwing rotten vegetables, dead animals, or stones at them.

THE DEATH PENALTY

The worst punishment was to be hanged, drawn, and quartered. This was the punishment for treason, or betraying one's country. Felons were dragged to a place of execution on a hurdle, a kind of sled, where they were hanged, disemboweled, and then taken down. While they were still alive, their innards were thrown into a fire, and their bodies were cut into quarters.

Burning at the stake was used across Europe to punish heresy, or wrong beliefs, and witchcraft. Burning ensured that the condemned had no body to take with them into the next life, and that no physical remnants of his or her body would serve as relics. Women were burned instead of being hanged, drawn, and quartered.

Most executions were hangings, but members of the nobility who were sentenced to death were beheaded rather than hanged.

BENEFIT OF CLERGY

It was possible to escape the death penalty for some crimes by claiming "benefit of clergy." Since medieval times the clergy were tried by church courts, which did not hand down the death penalty. In 1487 the right to be exempted from the death penalty was extended to all men who could read. The courts tested a felon's ability to read by asking him to read out a biblical verse, which came to be known as the "neck verse." Many illiterate felons learned the verse by heart to cheat death.

It was only possible to claim benefit of clergy once. The convicted were branded on the thumb for the first offense. If they were convicted again, they faced death. Some crimes were considered too serious to receive the benefit of clergy, including stabbing, horse theft, and burglary.

PRISON

Prison was a place where people were held until their trial. Prisons were very unpleasant places. One 17th-century observer wrote, "A prison is a grave to bury men alive.... It is a place that hath more diseases predominant in it than a pesthouse in the Plague-time." Prisons were open to the street, and the general public could come and observe the

inmates as a form of entertainment. Some prisoners managed to beg enough money from passers-by to buy their freedom.

In the later 16th century "houses of correction," also known as workhouses, were established for vagrants and prostitutes to teach them skills so that they could gain work that was legal. The inmates were forced to work at weaving and spinning.

PUBLIC EXECUTIONS

Trials and executions in London took place four times a year. The days of public hangings were holidays. They were popular days out and attracted crowds of tourists.

The spectacle began in the morning. The condemned person left the prison on a cart with the hangman and a chaplain, often sitting on his or her own coffin. Accompanied by a troop of soldiers, he or she traveled to the place of execution through crowds of people. On the way the condemned person might stop at a tavern and drink with the hangman or say prayers with the

priest. At the place of execution he or she had a chance to speak to the crowd (*see box p. 61*). Traditionally, the convict's speech was a confession of crimes and an expression of repentance. Then the condemned person was put in a noose, and the cart was driven off, leaving him or her to hang. The body was later taken down and buried.

A 16th-century engraving of Protestant prisoners in Newgate Prison, London. During the reign of Queen Mary I (ruled 1553–1558) 274 Protestants were burned at the stake for heresy.

TRANSPORTATION

In the 16th and 17th centuries transportation was the removal of undesirable people from society. They were mostly criminals, but in some cases dangerously sick people were also taken from Europe to the Americas, usually to an isolated island, to reduce the risk of an epidemic breaking out.

The English used transportation as an alternative to execution. Large-scale transportation began in 1663. Private merchants were expected to buy convicts at a price, which included the cost of their trial, confinement in prison, and the legal cost of their pardon. Shipped to the American colonies, convicts were sold into service for a term determined by their offense. This enterprise was profitable only if the convict was young and healthy. However, many were too old and sick to return the merchants' investment. In 1670 the colonies of Virginia and Maryland passed laws prohibiting transportation.

The second period of transportation began in 1718, when the English government transported criminals to other overseas colonies. This time transportation was not an attempt to recover the cost of the offenders' trial and imprisonment but simply to remove from society the growing criminal underclass.

SEE ALSO

DAILY LIFE

In the 16th and 17th centuries daily life in Europe varied according to different factors such as a person's age, status, gender, and religion. However, regardless of these distinctions, everyone lived in the shadow of death and disease.

During this period the Plague was the largest killer. Other illnesses such as pneumonia and smallpox also took many lives. Since no one had central heating, winter was a deadly season: Many people contracted respiratory infections that were often fatal. Without clean water or refrigeration the summers were also perilous: stomachaches and dysentery were common. However, widespread disease and the high death rate did not cause people to live somber lives. Dancing, music, religious festivals, and theatrical entertainment were popular among all sectors of society. By 1700 theater reached new heights of artistic development. Opera, a new musical form in the 16th century, also flourished.

Most people worked in agriculture, produced goods of some kind, or

Dutch artist Pieter Brueghel the Elder's **The Triumph of Death** *from 1562 conveys the 16th-century preoccupation with ever-present death.*

worked as servants in the households of wealthy people. During this period the number of towns and cities steadily increased. In the cities and towns artisans made goods, including textiles, clothing, and musical instruments. In rural areas peasants grew grain and raised animals for food, and used animal pelts for clothing. Aristocrats, who formed a small group in society, owned most of the land that peasants farmed and inhabited. They demanded rent from their tenants and often employed up to 40 servants in one household. Between 1500 and 1700 landowners increasingly fenced off their lands, denying peasants grazing rights.

DIFFERENT HOMES

Peasants usually lived in cottages with two rooms, one for cooking, eating, and working, and the other for sleeping. These cottages had a single hearth in the middle of one of the rooms where a fire provided warmth and light. With only a simple hole in the roof and no chimney, the cottages were very smoky. The better-off built fireplaces with chimneys, but most people had open fires and suffered from eye infections and smelled of wood smoke. Heating a house and keeping it supplied with water took a lot of time and energy. Only a few palaces had running water. Most people, usually women, fetched water for drinking and bathing from the river or a public well. Women often washed clothes and dishes near the water source. Nobles and wealthier professionals paid a water carrier.

Wealthy people sometimes decorated their homes with tapestries, religious icons, ornate furnishings, and paintings. However, even most wealthy households were sparsely furnished, and the few items a family owned were highly valued and passed from one generation to the next. For peasants

ANIMALS

In the 16th and 17th centuries nearly every aspect of daily life involved animals. They were raised for food and were used for farm labor. They also provided the raw materials for goods such as gloves, shoes, candles, quill pens, perfumes, and woolen textiles. Horses were the primary mode of transportation, and they were indispensable in warfare. Many leisure activities involved animals. A nobleman's pastimes consisted of hunting, hawking, riding, and occasionally watching animal baiting. This activity involved setting dogs on a larger creature such as a bear or a bull, which was often chained or otherwise handicapped. Baiting was especially popular in England, and dedicated amphitheaters staged the spectacles.

Some animals such as dogs or caged songbirds were kept as pets for companionship or because they had a pleasing appearance. The rise of overseas exploration also led to exotic animals such as parrots and monkeys becoming pets.

A 17th-century print showing animal baiting, a form of sport that involved dogs fighting bears, bulls, and other animals.

and other poorer people the bed was a family's most important possession and was usually inherited as an heirloom. The bedroom was also the most important and most carefully decorated room in a house: Nobles often entertained guests there and kept their treasured belongings around their beds.

BASIC NEEDS

In the courts and other wealthy households servants attended to their employers' most basic needs. For example, in the morning a nobleman would have servants to help him get dressed and to put on his makeup and perfume. Perfume was a very important part of a nobleman's grooming, because it disguised the effects of going for long periods without bathing. It was common practice to wash the hands and face but not the entire body. People usually cleaned their teeth after meals by washing their mouths out with wine. They then used a cloth or a special toothpick that some wore on a string around their neck.

People considered washing the entire body to be unhealthy. The drafty nature of the houses and the lack of hot running water increased the chances of catching a cold. The infrequency of bathing and the lack of running water meant that houses often had a bad odor. Wealthier people kept close-stools, an early toilet, in their bedroom or in a separate room near the bedroom. Monarchs often had a special servant, the Keeper of the Stool, who emptied his or her chamber pot. Servants and other people of lower status used outdoor communal pits in which they could relieve themselves.

FEASTING AND CELEBRATING

In the 16th and 17th centuries one sign of wealth was how much meat there was in a person's diet. Most people's diets consisted primarily of porridge and brown breads seasoned with raw garlic or onion. Pork, salted or smoked, was the cheapest and the most commonly eaten meat. Nobles could afford to eat all kinds of meat. At banquets they might eat the meat of an array of exotic animals such as boar, swan, peacock, and cormorant, a kind of seabird. It was common practice for everyone to abstain from eating meat on religious fast days scheduled by the church, such as

Spring by Flemish artist Abel Grimmer, painted in 1607. Daily life for peasants involved tending agricultural fields and working on their master's gardens.

WANDERERS AND VAGABONDS

In the 16th and 17th century many people moved from place to place seeking work or for various reasons lived outside settled communities. Vagabonds and homeless people wandered between towns in search of food and shelter. In England around 10 percent of the rural population and 20 percent of the urban population were homeless. Some people who were on the road for most of the year made enough money to sustain themselves, sometimes illegally. Merchants, peddlers, actors, and the gypsies who played music and told fortunes for money were engaged in lawful activity. Thieves, assassins, and gypsies who stole or sold stolen goods were perceived as dangerous criminals. Criminals and other outsiders lacked respectability in the eyes of society and relied on the fellowship they found within their own cultures. The world of lawlessness was a source of public fascination.

An engraving by Swiss artist Jost Amman dating from 1568. It shows a typical 16th-century peddler selling his wares.

Lent, the 40 days before Easter, and during other religious fast days.

The Christian calendar marked the passing of each year with the major holidays of Christmas and Easter and many other fast and feast days. The religious calendar coincided with seasonal changes. Farmers sheared sheep, harvested crops, and plowed their fields in accordance with the calendar of holy days. Everyone celebrated during carnival, the week before Lent. In cities and villages actors staged plays in the streets. The public participated in a theatrical game called a masquerade in which they wore disguises and played tricks on each other. One trick involved throwing eggs at people, some of which were perfumed and others of which were rotten. However, sometimes the celebrations got out of control, and violence erupted, primarily aimed at animals or outsiders such as Jews. For most people carnival was a relief from the rigid social order and the monotony of everyday life. After the Reformation Protestant states abolished many saints days and other special days in the church calendar, believing they encouraged idleness and superstition.

SEE ALSO

- Children
- Clocks and calendars
- Courts and courtiers
- Decorative arts
- Enclosure
- Environment
- Families
- Food and drink
- Houses and furniture
- Privacy and luxury
- Servants
- Social order
- Sports
- Wealth and poverty

TIMELINE

♦ **1492** Christopher Columbus lands in the Bahamas, claiming the territory for Spain.

♦ **1494** Charles VIII of France invades Italy, beginning four decades of Italian wars.

♦ **1494** The Treaty of Tordesillas divides the "new world" between Spain and Portugal.

♦ **1498** Portuguese navigator Vasco da Gama sails around Africa to reach Calicut, India.

♦ **1509** Dutch humanist scholar Desiderius Erasmus publishes *In Praise of Folly*, a satire on religion and society.

♦ **1511** The Portuguese capture Melaka in Southeast Asia.

♦ **1515** Francis I of France invades Italy, capturing Milan.

♦ **1516** Charles, grandson of Holy Roman emperor Maximilian I, inherits the Spanish throne as Charles I.

♦ **1517** The German monk Martin Luther nails his Ninety-five Theses to a church door in Wittenberg, Germany, setting the Reformation in motion.

♦ **1518** The Portuguese begin trading in slaves from Africa.

♦ **1519** Charles I of Spain is elected Holy Roman emperor as Charles V.

♦ **1519–1521** Spanish conquistador Hernán Cortés conquers Mexico for Spain.

♦ **1520** Suleyman the Magnificent becomes sultan of the Ottoman Empire.

♦ **1520** Portuguese navigator Ferdinand Magellan rounds the tip of South America and is the first European to sight the Pacific Ocean.

♦ **1521** Pope Leo X excommunicates Martin Luther.

♦ **1521** At the Diet of Worms, Luther refuses to recant his views. The Holy Roman emperor outlaws him.

♦ **1522** One of Magellan's ships completes the first circumnavigation of the globe.

♦ **1523** Gustav Vasa becomes king of Sweden and dissolves the Kalmar Union that had dominated Scandinavia.

♦ **1523–1525** Huldrych Zwingli sets up a reformed church in Zurich, Switzerland.

♦ **1525** Holy Roman Emperor Charles V defeats and captures Francis I of France at the Battle of Pavia.

♦ **1525** In Germany the Peasants' Revolt is crushed; its leaders, including the radical Thomas Münzer, are executed.

♦ **1525** William Tyndale translates the New Testament into English.

♦ **1526** Mongol leader Babur invades northern India and establishes the Mogul Empire.

♦ **1526** At the Diet of Speyer German princes are granted the authority to allow Lutheran teachings and worship in their own territories.

♦ **1526** Suleyman the Magnificent defeats Hungarian forces at the Battle of Mohács.

♦ **1527** Charles V's forces overrun Italy and sack Rome.

♦ **1529** In the Peace of Cambrai with Charles V, Francis I of France renounces all French claims in Italy temporarily confirming Spanish supremacy.

♦ **1529** The Ottoman sultan Suleyman the Magnificent besieges the city of Vienna.

♦ **1531** German Protestant princes form the Schmalkaldic League to defend themselves.

♦ **1531–1532** Spanish conquistador Francisco Pizarro conquers Peru for Spain by defeating the Inca Empire.

♦ **1532** Niccolò Machiavelli's *The Prince* is published.

♦ **1534** The earl of Kildare, Thomas Lord Offaly, leads a revolt against Henry VIII's rule in Ireland.

♦ **1534** Henry VIII of England breaks away from the authority of the pope and establishes the Church of England.

♦ **1534** Martin Luther publishes his German translation of the New Testament.

♦ **1535–1536** The city of Geneva adopts Protestantism and expels all Catholic clergy.

♦ **1536** Henry VIII orders the dissolution of the monasteries.

♦ **1536** John Calvin publishes his *Institutes of the Christian Religion*, which sets out central Protestant principles.

♦ **1539** Ignatius Loyola founds the Society of Jesus (Jesuits).

♦ **1541** John Calvin sets up a model Christian community in Geneva, Switzerland.

♦ **1542** Pope Paul III reestablishes the Inquisition, a medieval religious court designed to combat heresy.

♦ **1543** The Flemish anatomist Andreas Vesalius publishes his handbook of anatomy *On the Structure of the Human Body*.

♦ **1543** Polish astronomer Nicolaus Copernicus publishes *On the Revolutions of the Heavenly Orbs*, which challenged contemporary beliefs by describing a sun-centered universe.

♦ **1545** Pope Paul III organizes the Council of Trent to counter the threat of Protestantism and reinvigorate the church.

♦ **1547** Ivan IV (the Terrible) becomes czar of Russia.

♦ **1547** Charles V defeats the Schmalkaldic League at the Battle of Mühlberg.

♦ **1553** Mary I restores the Catholic church in England.

♦ **1555** In the Peace of Augsburg Charles V allows German princes to decide the religion in their territories.

♦ **1555** Charles V abdicates, dividing his vast lands between his brother Ferdinand and son Philip.

♦ **1558** On the death of Mary I, her half-sister Elizabeth I becomes queen of England.

♦ **1559** Elizabeth I restores the Church of England.

♦ **1559** Pope Paul IV institutes the Index of Prohibited Books.

♦ **1562** The Wars of Religion break out in France.

♦ **1563** The Council of Trent ends having clarified Catholic doctrine and laid the basis of the Counter Reformation.

♦ **1566** The Dutch begin a revolt against Spanish rule.

♦ **1569** Flemish cartographer Gerardus Mercator publishes a world map using a new method of projection.

♦ **1571** Philip II of Spain leads an allied European force to victory over the Ottomans at the naval Battle of Lepanto.

♦ **1572** French Catholics murder thousands of Protestants across France in the Saint Bartholomew's Day Massacre.

♦ **1579** Seven Dutch provinces form the Union of Utrecht to fight for independence from Spanish rule.

♦ **1582** The warlord Toyotomi Hideyoshi becomes effective ruler of Japan.

♦ **1588** Philip II launches the Armada invasion fleet against England, but it is destroyed.

♦ **1590** Toyotomi Hideyoshi expels Christian missionaries from Japan.

♦ **1593** The English playwright William Shakespeare publishes his first work, *Venus and Adonis* beginning his prolific and successful career in the theater.

♦ **1598** The Persian Safavid ruler Shah Abbas the Great moves his capital to Esfahan.

♦ **1598** In the Edict of Nantes Henry IV of France grants Huguenots considerable rights, bringing an end to the French Wars of Religion.

♦ **1600** The English East India Company is founded in London to control trade with India and East Asia.

♦ **1602** The Dutch government establishes the Dutch East India Company.

♦ **1603** In Japan Tokugawa Ieyasu unites the country under his rule as shogun, ushering in a age of peace and prosperity.

♦ **1603** James VI of Scotland also becomes king of England as James I on the death of Elizabeth I.

♦ **1605** The Gunpowder Plot: A group of Catholics including Guy Fawkes fail to blow up the English Parliament.

♦ **1607** Henry Hudson sails to the Barents Sea in search of a northeastern passage to Asia.

♦ **1607** John Smith founds the English colony of Jamestown in Virginia.

♦ **1611** James I's authorized Bible, the King James Version, is published.

♦ **1616** Cardinal Richelieu becomes the prime minister of France.

♦ **1618** The Defenestration of Prague marks the beginning of the Thirty Years' War.

♦ **1620** The *Mayflower* pilgrims found the colony of New Plymouth in Massachusetts.

♦ **1621** Huguenots (French Protestants) rebel against King Louis XIII of France.

♦ **1625** Charles I is crowned king of England.

♦ **1629** Charles I dissolves Parliament and rules independently until 1640.

♦ **1631** The Mogul Emperor Shah Jahan builds the Taj Mahal as a mausoleum for his wife Mumtaz.

♦ **1632** Galileo Galilei publishes his *Dialogue Concerning the Two Chief World Systems,* in which he supports Copernicus's views of a sun-centered universe.

♦ **1633** Galileo is tried for heresy and sentenced to house arrest by the Roman Inquisition.

♦ **1637–1638** After a rebellion led by Christians in Japan 37,000 Japanese Christians are executed and many Europeans expelled from the country.

♦ **1640** Portuguese peasants rebel against Spanish rule and declare John of Braganza their king. Portugal finally regains its independence in 1668.

♦ **1641** French philosopher René Descartes publishes one of his most important works, *Meditations on First Philosophy.*

♦ **1642** Civil war breaks out in England between the king and Parliament.

♦ **1642** Jules Mazarin follows Cardinal Richelieu to become prime minister of France.

♦ **1643** Louis XIV becomes king of France. During his reign France becomes powerful.

♦ **1648** The Thirty Years' War comes to an end with the Treaty of Westphalia.

♦ **1648–1653** The Fronde, a series of civil wars, breaks out in France.

♦ **1649** The English king Charles I is executed and England becomes a republic.

♦ **1652** England and the Dutch Republic clash in the first Anglo-Dutch Naval War.

♦ **1653** The English Puritan Oliver Cromwell dissolves Parliament and rules England as lord protector.

♦ **1660** The English Parliament restores Charles II as king.

♦ **1660** The Royal Society of London is founded to promote scientific enquiry.

♦ **1661** Louis XIV begins work on the palace of Versailles outside Paris.

♦ **1661** Manchu Emperor Kang-hsi comes to power in China. His long reign marks a golden age in Chinese history.

♦ **1665** The Great Plague in London kills around a thousand people every week.

♦ **1666** French minister Jean-Baptiste Colbert establishes the French Academy to promote the sciences.

♦ **1666** The Great Fire of London destroys a large part of the English capital.

♦ **1670** The English Hudson's Bay Company is founded to occupy lands and trade in North America.

♦ **1678** English Puritan writer John Bunyan publishes his hugely popular allegorical book *Pilgrim's Progress.*

♦ **1683** The Turkish Ottoman army besieges Vienna for the second time.

♦ **1685** Louis XIV revokes the Edict of Nantes, depriving French Protestants of all religious and civil liberties. Hundreds of thousands of Huguenots flee France.

♦ **1688** In the Glorious Revolution the Protestant Dutch leader, William of Orange, is invited to replace James II as king of England.

♦ **1689** The Bill of Rights establishes a constitutional monarchy in England. William III and his wife Mary II jointly rule England and Scotland.

♦ **1694** The Bank of England is founded in London.

♦ **1699** Turks withdraw from Austria and Hungary.

♦ **1700–1721** The Great Northern War between Sweden and Russia and its allies weakens Swedish power.

♦ **1701** The War of the Spanish Succession breaks out over the vacant Spanish throne.

♦ **1704** Isaac Newton publishes his book *Optics* on the theory of light and color.

♦ **1707** The Act of Union unites England and Scotland. The seat of Scottish government is moved to London.

♦ **1712** Peter the Great makes Saint Petersburg the new capital of Russia, beginning a period of westernization.

♦ **1713–1714** The treaties of Utrecht are signed by England and France, ending the War of the Spanish Succession.

♦ **1715** The sun king King Louis XIV of France dies, marking the end of a golden age in French culture.

GLOSSARY

Absolutism
A system of government in which far-reaching power is held by a monarch or ruler over his or her subjects.

Alchemy
A tradition of investigative thought that tried to explain the relationship between humanity and the universe and exploit it, for example, by finding a way to turn base metal into gold.

Baroque
An artistic style originating in the 17th century characterized by dramatic effects and ornamentation, which aimed to evoke a strong emotional response.

Calvinists
Followers of the French Protestant reformer John Calvin. Calvinism emphasized the sovereignty of God and predestination—the idea that that God decided in advance who would gain eternal life.

Counter Reformation
The Catholic church's efforts to reinvigorate itself, bring an end to abuses, clarify its teachings, and prevent the spread of Protestantism.

Diet
An assembly of the rulers of the Holy Roman Empire, who gathered to pass laws and make important decisions.

Doctrine
A specific principle or belief, or system of beliefs, taught by a religious faith.

Elector
A leading landowner in the Holy Roman Empire who had a vote in the election of the Holy Roman emperor.

Enclosure
A process by which major landowners extended their holdings across common land.

Excommunication
A punishment in which a person was banned from taking part in the rites of the Catholic church.

Franciscans
Members of a Catholic religious order founded in the early 13th century by Saint Francis of Assisi.

Guild
An association of merchants, professionals, or craftsmen organized to protect the interests of its members and to regulate the quality and cost of their services.

Heresy
A belief that is contrary to the teachings of a religious faith.

Huguenots
The name given to Calvinists in France.

Humanism
An academic approach based on the study of "humanities"—that is, ancient Greek and Roman texts, history, and philosophy—which stressed the importance of developing rounded, cultured individuals.

Iconoclasm
The destruction of religious objects, usually by those who disapproved of the use of images in worship.

Indulgences
The cancelation or reduction of punishments for sins granted by the Catholic church in return for good works or money.

Inquisition
A powerful medieval religious court that was revived by the Catholic church in the 16th century to stamp out ideas contrary to Catholic teachings.

Janissaries
Members of an elite infantry corps in the Ottoman army.

Jesuits
Members of a Catholic order founded in the 16th century by Ignatius Loyola. They were famous for their work as educators and missionaries.

Laity or laypeople
Members of a religious faith who are not clergy.

Lutherans
Followers of the German Protestant reformer Martin Luther. He protested against abuses in the Catholic church and argued that the scriptures, not church traditions, were the ultimate religious authority.

Mass or Eucharist
A key Christian sacrament of thanksgiving for the sacrifice of Jesus's life celebrated with wine and bread representing his body and blood.

Mercantilism
An economic system under which a government regulated manufacturing and trade in the belief that high exports and low imports would enrich the country's treasury and make the state powerful.

Mercenary
A soldier who fights for any employer in return for wages.

Papacy
The pope and his advisers in Rome who govern the Catholic church.

Patriarch
The title given to Orthodox church leaders: The most important patriarchs were the bishops of Antioch, Rome, Alexandria, Constantinople, and Jerusalem.

Patron
Someone who orders and pays for a work of art or supports, usually financially, the work of an artist or thinker.

Protestant
Someone who follows one of the Christian churches set up during the Reformation in reaction to the corruption of the Catholic church.

Sacrament
An important Christian ritual, or ceremony, such as Mass or baptism. The number and nature of the sacraments were issues of major debate during the Reformation.

Secular
A term to describe something nonreligious as opposed to something religious.

Theology
The study of religion.

Tithe
A tax of one-tenth of a person's annual produce or income payable to the church.

Usury
The practice of making a dishonest profit, such as charging high interest on a loan, which was considered sinful by the medieval church.

Vernacular
The everyday language spoken by the people of a country or region, rather than a literary or formal language such as Latin.

FURTHER READING

Barry, J., M. Hester, and G. Roberts (eds.). *Witchcraft in Early Modern Europe: Studies in Culture and Belief.* New York: Cambridge University Press, 1996.

Black, C. F. *Church, Religion, and Society in Early Modern Italy.* New York: Palgrave, 2001.

Boorstin, Daniel J. *The Discoverers.* New York: Harry N. Abrams, 1991.

Collinson, Patrick. *The Reformation: A History.* New York: Modern Library, 2004.

Darby, G. (ed.). *The Origins and Development of the Dutch Revolt.* New York: Routledge, 2001.

Dixon, C. S. *The Reformation in Germany.* Malden, Mass.: Blackwell Publishers, 2002.

Duffy, Eamon. *Saints and Sinners: A History of the Popes.* New Haven, Conn.: Yale University Press, 1997.

Elliott , J. H. *Europe Divided 1559–1598.* Second edition, Malden, Mass.: Blackwell Publishers, 2000.

Gäbler, U., and R.C.L. Gritsch (trans.). *Huldrych Zwingli: His Life and Work.* Philadelphia: Fortress Press, 1998.

Goodwin, Jason. *Lords of the Horizons: A History of the Ottoman Empire.* New York: Henry Holt, 1999.

Henry, J. *The Scientific Revolution and the Origins of Modern Science.* Second edition, New York: Palgrave, 2001.

Jaffer, Amin, and Anna Jackson (eds.). *Encounters: The Meeting of Asia and Europe 1500–1800.* New York: Harry N. Abrams, 2004.

Jewell, Helen M. *Education in Early Modern England.* New York: St. Martin's Press, 1998.

Jones, M. D. W. *The Counter Reformation: Religion and Society in Early Modern Europe.* New York: Cambridge University Press, 1995.

Klein, Herbert S. *The Atlantic Slave Trade.* New York: Cambridge University Press, 1999.

Kuhn, Thomas S. *The Copernican Revolution.* New York: MJF Books, 1997.

Lane, Kris. *Pillaging the Empire: Piracy in the Americas, 1500–1750.* Armok, NY: M. E. Sharpe, 1998.

Lindberg, Carter (ed.). *The European Reformation Sourcebook.* Malden, Mass.: Blackwell Publishers, 1999.

MacCulloch, Diarmaid. *The Reformation: A History.* New York: Viking Press, 2004.

Marius, R. *Martin Luther: The Christian between God and Death.* Cambridge, Mass.: Belknap Press, 1999.

McGrath, A. E. *Reformation Thought.* Third edition, Malden, Mass.: Blackwell Publishers, 1999.

Oakley, S. P. *War and Peace in the Baltic 1560–1790.* New York: Routledge, 1992.

Porter, Roy. *The Greatest Benefit to Mankind: Medical History of Humanity.* New York: W. W. Norton, 1998.

Rawlings, Helen. *The Spanish Inquisition.* Malden, Mass.: Blackwell Publishers, 2005.

Renaissance. Danbury, Connecticut: Grolier, 2002.

Roth, Mitchel P. *Crime and Punishment: A History of the Criminal Justice System.* Belmont, CA: Thomson Wadsworth, 2005.

Russell-Wood, A. J. R. *The Portuguese Empire, 1415–1808: A World on the Move.* Baltimore, MD: Johns Hopkins University Press, 1998.

Schama, Simon. *The Embarrassment of Riches: Dutch Culture in the Golden Age.* New York: Vintage Books, 1997.

Stoyle, John. *Europe Unfolding 1648–1688.* Second edition, Malden, Mass.: Blackwell Publishers, 2000.

Taylor, Alan. *American Colonies: The Settlement of North America to 1800.* New York: Penguin Books, 2003.

Tracy, J. D. *Europe's Reformations 1450–1650.* Lanham: Rowman & Littlefield, 1999.

Walvin, James. *The Quakers: Money and Morals.* London: John Murray, 1997.

Ware, Timothy. *The Orthodox Church.* New York: Penguin Books, 2004.

Wilson, P. H. *The Holy Roman Empire, 1495–1806.* New York: St. Martin's Press, 1999.

WEBSITES

BBC Online: History
www.bbc.co.uk/history

British Civil Wars, Commonwealth, and Protectorate 1638–1660
www.british-civil-wars.co.uk

Catholic Encyclopedia
www.newadvent.org/cathen/

Database of Reformation Artists
www.artcyclopedia.com/index.html

History of Protestantism
www.doctrine.org/history/

The Library of Economics and Liberty
www.econlib.org

National Gallery of Art
www.nga.gov

National Maritime Museum, Greenwich
www.nmm.ac.uk

Reformation History
www.historychannel.com

SET INDEX

PICTURE CREDITS